Henry Longueville Mansel

The Philosophy of the Conditioned

Comprising some remarks on Sir William Hamilton's philosophy, and on Mr. J.S. Mill's examination of that philosophy

Henry Longueville Mansel

The Philosophy of the Conditioned
Comprising some remarks on Sir William Hamilton's philosophy, and on Mr. J.S. Mill's examination of that philosophy

ISBN/EAN: 9783337068356

Printed in Europe, USA, Canada, Australia, Japan

Cover: Foto ©Thomas Meinert / pixelio.de

More available books at **www.hansebooks.com**

THE PHILOSOPHY OF THE CONDITIONED

*Comprising some Remarks on Sir William Hamilton's Philosophy
and on Mr. J. S. Mill's Examination of that Philosophy*

BY H. L. MANSEL, B.D.

WAYNFLETE PROFESSOR OF MORAL AND METAPHYSICAL PHILOSOPHY IN THE
UNIVERSITY OF OXFORD

ALEXANDER STRAHAN, PUBLISHER
LONDON AND NEW YORK
1866

MUIR AND PATERSON, PRINTERS, EDINBURGH.

PREFACE.

THE circumstance that the following remarks were originally published as an anonymous article in a Review, will best explain the style in which they are written. Absence from England prevented me from becoming acquainted with Mr. Mill's *Examination of Sir William Hamilton's Philosophy* till some time after its publication; and when I was requested to undertake the task of reviewing it, I was still ignorant of its contents. On proceeding to fulfil my engagement, I soon discovered, not only that the character of the book was very different from what the author's reputation had led me to expect, but also that my task would be one, not merely of criticism, but, in some degree, of self-defence. The remarks on myself, coming from a writer of Mr. Mill's ability and reputation, were such as I could not pass over without notice; while, at the same time, I felt that my principal duty in this instance was the defence of one who was no longer living to defend himself. Under these circumstances, the best course appeared to be, to devote the greater portion of my article to an exposition and vindication of Sir W. Hamilton's teaching; and, in the additional remarks which it was necessary to make on the more personal part of the controversy, to speak of myself in the third person, as

I should have spoken of any other writer. The form thus adopted has been retained in the present republication, though the article now appears with the name of its author.

My original intention of writing a review of the entire book was necessarily abandoned as soon as I became acquainted with its contents. To have done justice to the whole subject, or to Mr. Mill's treatment of it, would have required a volume nearly as large as his own. I therefore determined to confine myself to the *Philosophy of the Conditioned*, both as the most original and important portion of Sir W. Hamilton's teaching, and as that which occupies the first place in Mr. Mill's *Examination*.

THE PHILOSOPHY OF THE CONDITIONED.

THE reader of Plato's *Republic* will readily recall to mind that wonderful passage at the end of the sixth book, in which the philosopher, under the image of geometrical lines, exhibits the various relations of the intelligible to the sensible world; especially his lofty aspirations with regard to "that second segment of the intelligible world, which reason of itself grasps by the power of dialectic, employing hypotheses, not as principles, but as veritable hypotheses, that is to say, as steps and starting-points, in order that it may ascend as *far as the unconditioned* (μέχρι τοῦ ἀνυποθέτου), to the first principle of the universe, and having grasped this, may then lay hold of the principles next adjacent to it, and so go down to the end, using no sensible aids whatever, but employing abstract forms throughout, and terminating in forms."

This quotation is important for our present purpose in two ways. In the first place, it may serve, at the outset of our remarks, to propitiate those plain-spoken English critics who look upon new terms in philosophy with the same suspicion with which Jack Cade regarded "a noun and a verb, and such abominable words as no Christian ear can endure to hear," by showing that the head and front of our offending, "the Unconditioned," is no modern invention of Teutonic barbarism, but sanctioned even by the Attic elegance of a Plato. And in the second place, it contains almost a history in miniature of the highest speculations of philosophy, both in earlier and in later times, and points out, with a clearness and precision the more valuable because uninfluenced by recent controversies, the exact field on which the philosophies of the Conditioned and the Unconditioned come into collision, and the nature of the problem which they both approach from opposite sides.

What is the meaning of this problem, the solution of which Plato proposes as the highest aim of philosophy—"to ascend to the unconditioned, and thence to deduce the universe of conditioned existence?" The problem has assumed different forms at different times : at present we must content ourselves with stating it in that in which it will most naturally suggest itself to a student of modern philosophy, and in which it has the most direct bearing on the subject of the present article.

All consciousness must in the first instance present itself as a relation between two constituent parts, the person who is conscious, and the thing, whatever it may be, of which he is conscious. This contrast has been indicated, directly or indirectly, by various names—mind and matter ; person and thing ; subject and object ; or, lastly, in the distinction, most convenient for philosophy, however uncouth in sound, between self and not self—the *ego* and the *non-ego*. In order to be conscious at all, I must be conscious of something : consciousness thus presents itself as the product of two factors, *I* and *something*. The problem of the unconditioned is, briefly stated, to reduce these two factors to one.

For it is manifest that, so long as they remain two, we have no unconditioned, but a pair of conditioned existences. If the *something* of which I am conscious is a separate reality, having qualities and modes of action of its own, and thereby determining, or contributing to determine, the form which my consciousness of it shall take, my consciousness is thereby conditioned, or partly dependent on something beyond itself. It is no matter, in this respect, whether the influence is direct or indirect—whether, for instance, I see a material tree, or only the mental image of a tree. If the nature of the thing in any degree determines the character of the image—if the visible form of a tree is different from that of a house because the tree itself is different from the house, my consciousness is, however remotely, influenced by something different from itself, the *ego* by the *non-ego*. And on the other hand, if I, who am conscious, am a real being, distinct from the things of which I am conscious—if the conscious mind has a constitution and laws of its own by which it acts, and if the mode of its consciousness is in any degree determined by those laws, the *non-ego* is so far conditioned by the *ego;* the thing which I see is not seen absolutely and *per se*, but in a form partly dependent upon the laws of my vision.

7 The first step towards the reduction of these two factors to one may obviously be made in three different ways. Either the

ego may be represented as a mode of the *non-ego*, or the *non-ego* of the *ego*, or both of a *tertium quid*, distinct from either. In other words: it may be maintained, *first*, that matter is the only real existence; mind and all the phenomena of consciousness being really the result solely of material laws; the brain, for example, secreting thought as the liver secretes bile; and the distinct personal existence of which I am apparently conscious being only the result of some such secretion. This is *Materialism*, which has then to address itself to the further problem, to reduce the various phenomena of matter to some one absolutely first principle on which everything else depends. Or it may be maintained, *secondly*, that mind is the only real existence; the intercourse which we apparently have with a material world being really the result solely of the laws of our mental constitution. This is *Idealism,* which again has next to attempt to reduce the various phenomena to some one immaterial principle. Or it may be maintained, *thirdly,* that real existence is to be sought neither in mind as mind nor in matter as matter; that both classes of phenomena are but qualities or modes of operation of something distinct from both, and on which both alike are dependent. Hence arises a third form of philosophy, which, for want of a better name, we will call *Indifferentism,* as being a system in which the characteristic differences of mind and matter are supposed to disappear, being merged in something higher than both.

In using the two former of these terms, we are not speaking of Materialism and Idealism as they have always actually manifested themselves, but only of the distinguishing principle of these systems when pushed to its extreme result. It is quite possible to be a materialist or an idealist with respect to the immediate phenomena of consciousness, without attempting a philosophy of the Unconditioned at all. But it is also possible, and in itself natural, when such a philosophy is attempted, to attempt it by means of the same method which has approved itself in relation to subordinate inquiries; to make the relation between the human mind and its objects the type and image of that between the universe and its first principle. And such attempts have actually been made, both on the side of Materialism and on that of Idealism; and probably would be made oftener, did not counteracting causes frequently hinder the logical development of speculative principles.

In modern times, and under Christian influences, these several systems are almost necessarily identified with inquiries concerning the existence and nature of God. The influence of Christianity has been indirectly felt, even in speculations prosecuted in apparent independence of it; and the admission of an absolute first principle of all things distinct from God, or the acknowledgment of a God separate from or derived from the first principle of all things, is an absurdity which, since the prevalence of Christianity, has become almost impossible, even to antichristian systems of thought. In earlier times, indeed, this union of philosophy with theology was by no means so imperative. A philosophy like that of Greece, which inherited its speculations from a poetical theogony, would see no difficulty in attributing to the god or gods of its religious belief a secondary and derived existence, dependent on some higher and more original principle, and in separating that principle itself from all immediate connection with religion. It was possible to assume, with the Ionian, a material substance, or, with the Eleatic, an indifferent abstraction, as the first principle of things, without holding that principle to be God, or, as the only alternative, denying the existence of a God; and thus, as Aristotle* has observed, theologians endeavoured to evade the consequences of their abstract principles, by attributing to the chief good a later and derived existence, as the poets supposed the supreme God to be of younger birth than

* *Metaph.*, xiv. 4.

night and chaos and sea and sky. But to a Christian philosophy, or to a philosophy in any way influenced by Christianity, this method of evasion is no longer possible. If all conditioned existence is dependent on some one first and unconditioned principle, either that principle must be identified with God, or our philosophical speculations must fall into open and avowed atheism.

But at this point the philosophical inquiry comes in contact with another line of thought, suggested by a different class of the facts of consciousness. As a religious and moral being, man is conscious of a relation of a personal character, distinct from any suggested by the phenomena of the material world,—a relation to a supreme Personal Being, the object of his religious worship, and the source and judge of his moral obligations and conduct. To adopt the name of God in an abstract speculation merely as a conventional denomination for the highest link in the chain of thought, and to believe in Him for the practical purposes of worship and obedience, are two very different things; and for the latter, though not for the former, the conception of God as a Person is indispensable. Were man a being of pure intellect, the problem of the Unconditioned would be divested of its chief difficulty; but he is also a being of religious and moral faculties, and these also have a claim to be satisfied by any valid solution of the problem. Hence the question assumes another and a more complex form. How is the one absolute existence, to which philosophy aspires, to be identified with the personal God demanded by our religious feelings?

Shall we boldly assume that the problem is already solved, and that the personal God is the very Unconditioned of which we were in search? This is to beg the question, not to answer it. Our conception of a personal being, derived as it is from the immediate consciousness of our own personality, seems, on examination, to involve conditions incompatible with the desired assumption. Personal agency, similar to our own, seems to point to something very different from an absolutely first link in a chain of phenomena. Our actions, if not determined, are at least influenced by motives; and the motive is a prior link in the chain, and a condition of the action. Our actions, moreover, take place in time; and time, as we conceive it, cannot be regarded as an absolute blank, but as a condition in which phenomena take place as past, present, and future. Every act taking place in time implies something antecedent to itself; and this something, be it what it may, hinders us from regarding the subsequent act as absolute and unconditioned. Nay, even time itself, apart from the phenomena which it implies, has the same character. If an act cannot take place except in time, time is the condition of its taking place. To conceive the unconditioned, as the first link in a chain of conditioned consequences, it seems necessary that we should conceive something out of time, yet followed by time; standing at the beginning of all duration and succession, having no antecedent, but followed by a series of consequents.

Philosophical theologians have been conscious of this difficulty, almost from the earliest date at which philosophy and Christian theology came in contact with each other. From a number of testimonies of similar import, we select one or two of the most striking. Of the Divine Nature, Gregory Nyssen says: "It is neither in place nor in time, but before these and above these in an unspeakable manner, contemplated itself by itself, through faith alone; neither measured by ages, nor moving along with times."* "In the changes of things," says Augustine, "you will find a past and a future; in God you will find a present where past and future cannot be."† "Eternity," says Aquinas, "has no succession, but exists all together."‡ Among divines of the Church of England, we quote two names

* *C. Eunom.*, i., p. 98, Ed. Gretser.
† *In Joann. Evang.*, tract. xxxvii. 10.
‡ *Summa*, pars. i., qu. x., art. 1.

only, but those of the highest :—"The duration of eternity," says Bishop Pearson, " is completely indivisible and all at once ; so that it is ever present, and excludes the other differences of time, past and future."*
And Barrow enumerates among natural modes of being and operation far above our reach, " God's eternity without succession," coupling it with " His prescience without necessitation of events."† But it is needless to multiply authorities for a doctrine so familiar to every student of theology.

Thus, then, our two lines of thought have led us to conclusions which, at first sight, appear to be contradictory of each other. To be conceived as unconditioned, God must be conceived as exempt from action in time :

---

* *Minor Theol. Works*, vol. i., p. 105.
† Sermon on the Unsearchableness of God's Judgments.

to be conceived as a person, if His personality resembles ours, He must be conceived as acting in time. Can these two conclusions be reconciled with each other; and if not, which of them is to be abandoned? The true answer to this question is, we believe, to be found in a distinction which some recent critics regard with very little favour, —the distinction between Reason and Faith; between the power of *conceiving* and that of *believing*. We cannot, in our present state of knowledge, reconcile these two conclusions; yet we are not required to abandon either. We cannot conceive the manner in which the unconditioned and the personal are united in the Divine Nature; yet we may believe that, in some manner unknown to us, they are so united. To conceive the union of two attributes in one object of thought, I must be able to conceive them as united in some particular manner : when this cannot be done, I may nevertheless believe *that* the union is possible, though I am unable to conceive *how* it is possible. The problem is thus represented as one of those Divine mysteries, the character of which is clearly and well described in the language of Leibnitz :—" Il en est de même des autres mystères, où les esprits modérés trouveront toujours une explication suffisante pour croire, et jamais autant qu'il en faut pour comprendre. Il nous suffit d'un certain *ce que c'est* (τί ἐστι) mais le *comment* (πῶς) nous passe, et ne nous est point nécessaire."*

* *Théodicée, Discours de la Conformité de la Foi avec la Raison*, § 56. Leibnitz, it will be observed, uses the expression *pour comprendre*, for which, in the preceding remarks, we have substituted *to conceive*. The change has been made intentionally, on account

But this distinction involves a further consequence. If the mysteries of the Divine Nature are not apprehended by reason as existing in a particular manner (in which case they would be mysteries no longer), but are accepted by faith as existing in some manner unknown to us, it follows that we do not know God as He is in His absolute nature, but only as He is imperfectly repre-

---

of an ambiguity in the former word. Sometimes it is used, as Leibnitz here uses it, to denote an apprehension of the manner in which certain attributes can coexist in an object. But sometimes (to say nothing of other senses) it is used to signify a complete knowledge of an object in all its properties and their consequences, such as it may be questioned whether we have of any object whatever. This ambiguity, which has been the source of much confusion and much captious criticism, is well pointed out by Norris in his *Reason and Faith* (written in reply to Toland), p. 118, Ed. 1697 : " When we say that *above reason* is when we do not comprehend or perceive the truth of a thing, this must not be meant of not comprehending the truth in its whöle latitude and extent, so that as many truths should be said to be above reason as we cannot

The Philosophy of the Conditioned. 21

sented by those qualities in His creatures which are analogous to, but not identical with, His own. If, for example, we had a knowledge of the Divine Personality as it is in itself, we should know it as existing in a certain manner compatible with unconditioned action; and this knowledge of the manner would at once transform our conviction from an act of faith to a conception of

---

thus thoroughly comprehend and pursue throughout all their consequences and relations to other truths (for then almost everything would be above reason), but only of not comprehending the union or connection of those immediate ideas of which the proposition supposed to be above reason consists." *Comprehension*, as thus explained, answers exactly to the ordinary logical use of the term *conception*, to denote the combination of two or more attributes in an unity of representation. In the same sense, M. Peisse, in the preface to his translation of Hamilton's *Fragments*, p. 98, says,— " Comprendre, c'est voir un terme en rapport avec un autre; c'est voir comme un ce qui est donné comme multiple." This is exactly the sense in which Hamilton himself uses the word *conception*. (See *Reid's Works*, p. 377.)

reason. If, on the other hand, the only personality of which we have a positive knowledge is our own, and if our own personality can only be conceived as conditioned in time, it follows that the Divine Personality, in so far as it is exempt from conditions, does not resemble the only personality which we directly know, and is not adequately represented by it. This necessitates a confession, which, like the distinction which gives rise to it, has been vehemently condemned by modern critics, but which has been concurred in with singular unanimity by earlier divines of various ages and countries,—the confession that the knowledge which man in this life can have of God is not a knowledge of the Divine Nature as it is in itself, but only of that nature as imperfectly represented through analogous qualities in the creature.

Were it not that this doctrine has been frequently denounced of late as an heretical novelty, we should hardly have thought it necessary to cite authorities in proof of its antiquity and catholicity. As it is, we will venture to produce a few only out of many, selecting not always the most important, but those which can be best exhibited *verbatim* in a short extract.

CHRYSOSTOM.—*De Incompr. Dei Natura*, Hom. i. 3: "*That* God is everywhere, I know; and *that* He is wholly everywhere, I know; but the *how*, I know not: *that* He is without beginning, ungenerated and eternal, I know; but the *how*, I know not."

BASIL.—Ep. ccxxxiv.: "That God is, I know; but what is His essence I hold to be above reason. How then am I saved? By faith; and faith is competent to know that God is, not what He is."

GREGORY NAZIANZEN.—Orat. xxxiv.: "A theologian among the Greeks [Plato] has said in his philosophy, that to conceive God is difficult, to express Him is impossible.

... But I say that it is impossible to express Him, and more impossible to conceive Him." [Compare Patrick, *Works*, vol. iii., p. 39.]

CYRIL OF JERUSALEM.—Catech. vi. 2 : " We declare not what God is, but candidly confess that we know not accurately concerning Him. For in those things which concern God, it is great knowledge to confess our ignorance."

AUGUSTINE.—Enarr. in Psalm. lxxxv. 8 : "God is ineffable; we more easily say what He is not than what He is." Serm. cccxli.: "I call God just, because in human words I find nothing better; for He is beyond justice. . . . What then is worthily said of God? Some one, perhaps, may reply and say, *that He is just.* But another, with better understanding, may say that even this word is surpassed by His excellence, and that even this is said of Him unworthily, though it be said fittingly according to human capacity."

CYRIL OF ALEXANDRIA.—*In Joann. Evang.*, l. ii., c. 5 : "For those things which are spoken concerning it [the Divine Nature] are not spoken as they are in very truth, but as the tongue of man can interpret, and as man can hear; for he who sees in an enigma also speaks in an enigma."

DAMASCENUS.—*De Fide Orthod.*, i. 4 : "That God is,

is manifest; but what He is in His essence and nature is utterly incomprehensible and unknown."

AQUINAS.—*Summa*, pars. i., qu. xiii., art. 1: " We cannot so name God that the name which denotes Him shall express the Divine Essence as it is, in the same way as the name *man* expresses in its signification the essence of man as it is." *Ibid.*, art. 5 : " When the name *wise* is said of a man, it in a manner describes and comprehends the thing signified: not so, however, when it is said of God ; but it leaves the thing signified as uncomprehended and exceeding the signification of the name. Whence it is evident that this name *wise* is not said in the same manner of God and of man. The same is the case with other names; whence no name can be predicated univocally of God and of creatures; yet they are not predicated merely equivocally. . . . We must say, then, that such names are said of God and of creatures according to analogy, that is, proportion."

HOOKER.—*Ecc. Pol.*, I., ii. 2.—" Dangerous it were for the feeble brain of man to wade far into the doings of the Most High; whom although to know be life, and joy to make mention of His name, yet our soundest knowledge is to know that we know Him not as indeed He is, neither can know Him."

USHER.—*Body of Divinity*, p. 45, Ed. 1645: "Neither is it [the wisdom of God] communicated to any creature, neither can be; for it is unconceivable, as the very essence of God Himself is unconceivable, and unspeakable as it is."

LEIGHTON.—Theol. Lect. XXI., *Works*, vol. iv., p. 327, Ed. 1830: "Though in the schools they distinguish the Divine attributes or excellences, and that by no means improperly, into communicable and incommunicable; yet we ought so to guard this distinction, as always to remember that those which are called communicable, when applied to God, are not only to be understood in a manner incommunicable and quite peculiar to Himself, but also, that in Him they are in reality infinitely different [in the original, *aliud omnino, immensum aliud*] from those virtues, or rather, in a matter where the disparity of the subjects is so very great, those shadows of virtues that go under the same name, either in men or angels."

PEARSON.—*Minor Theol. Works*, vol. i., p. 13: "God in Himself is an absolute being, without any relation to creatures, for He was from eternity without any creature, and could, had He willed, be to eternity without creature. But God cannot naturally be known by us otherwise than by relation to creatures, as, for example, under the aspect of dominion, or of cause, or in some other relation." *

BEVERIDGE.—*On the Thirty-nine Articles*, p. 16, Ed. 1846 : "But seeing the properties of God do not so much denote what God is, as what we apprehend Him to be in Himself; when the properties of God are predicated one of another, one thing in God is not predicated of another, but our apprehensions of the same thing are predicated one of another."

LESLIE.—*Method with the Deists*, p. 63, Ed. 1745 : "What we call *faculties* in the soul, we call *Persons* in the Godhead; because there are personal actions attributed to each of them. . . . And we have no other word whereby to express it; we speak it after the manner of men; nor could we understand if we heard any of those unspeakable words which express the Divine Nature in its proper essence; therefore we must make allowances, and great ones, when we apply words of our nature to the Infinite and Eternal Being." *Ibid.*, p. 64 : "By the

---

* Bishop Pearson's language is yet more explicit in another passage of the same work, which we give in the original Latin :— "Non dantur pro hoc statu nomina quæ Deum significant quidditative. Patet; quia nomina sunt conceptuum. Non autem dantur in hoc statu conceptus quidditativi de Deo."—(P. 136.)

word *Person*, when applied to God (for want of a proper word whereby to express it), we must mean something infinitely different from personality among men."

The system of theology represented by these extracts may, as we think, be fairly summed up as follows : We believe that God in His own nature is absolute and unconditioned; but we can only positively conceive Him by means of relations and conditions suggested by created things. We believe that His own nature is simple and uniform, admitting of no distinction between various attributes, nor between any attribute and its subject; but we can conceive Him only by means of various attributes, distinct from the subject and from each other.* We believe that in

---

* This will be found most distinctly stated in the context of the extract from Beveridge, and in the citations from St. Augustine given in his notes; to which may be added the following from *De Trinitate*, vi. 7 :—" Deus vero multipliciter quidem

The Philosophy of the Conditioned. 29

His own nature He is exempt from all relations of time; but we can conceive Him only by means of ideas and terms which imply temporal relations, a past, a present, and a future.* Our thought, then, must not be taken as the measure and limit of our belief: we think by means of relations and conditions derived from created things; we believe in an Absolute Being, in whose

---

dicitur magnus, bonus, sapiens, beatus, verus, et quidquid aliud non indigne dici videtur; sed eadem magnitudo ejus est quæ sapientia, non enim mole magnus est, sed virtute; et eadem bonitas quæ sapientia et magnitudo, et eadem veritas quæ illa omnia: et non est ibi aliud beatum esse et aliud magnum, aut sapientem, aut verum, aut bonum esse, aut omnino ipsum esse."

* Compare the remarkable words of Bishop Beveridge, *l. c.*, "And therefore, though I cannot apprehend His mercy to Abel in the beginning of the world, and His mercy to me now, but as two distinct expressions of His mercy, yet as they are in God, they are but one and the same act,—as they are in God, I say, who is not measured by time, as our apprehensions of Him are, but is Himself eternity; a centre without a circumference, eternity without time."

nature these conditions and relations, in some manner unknown to us, disappear in a simple and indivisible unity.

The most important feature of this philosophical theology, and the one which exhibits most clearly the practical difference between reason and faith, is that, in dealing with theoretical difficulties, it does not appeal to our knowledge, but to our ignorance: it does not profess to offer a definite solution; it only tells us that we might find one if we knew all. It does not profess, for example, to solve the apparent contradiction between God's foreknowledge and man's free will; it does not say, "This is the way in which God foreknows, and in this way His foreknowledge is reconcileable with human freedom;" it only says, "The contradiction is apparent, but need not be real. Freedom is incompatible with God's foreknowledge, only on the supposition that God's foreknowledge is like man's : if we knew exactly how the one differs from the other, we might be able to see that what is incompatible with the one is not so with the other. We cannot solve the difficulty, but we can believe that there is a solution."

It is this open acknowledgment of our ignorance of the highest things which makes this system of philosophy distasteful to many minds : it is the absence of any similar acknowledgment which forms the attraction and the seductiveness of Pantheism in one way, and of Positivism in another. The pantheist is not troubled with the difficulty of reconciling the philosophy of the absolute with belief in a personal God ; for belief in a personal God is no part of his creed. Like the Christian, he may profess to acknowledge a first principle, one, and simple, and indivisible, and unconditioned; but he has no need to give to this principle the name of God, or to invest it with such attributes as are necessary to satisfy man's religious wants. His God (so far as he acknowledges one at all) is not the first principle and cause of all things, but the aggregate of the whole—an universal substance underlying the world of phenomena, or an universal process, carried on in and by the changes of things. Hence, as Aristotle said of the Eleatics, that, by asserting all things to be one, they annihilated causation, which is the production of one thing from another, so it may be said of the various schools of Pantheism, that, by maintaining all things to be God, they evade rather than solve the great problem of philosophy, that of the relation between God and His creatures. The positivist, on the other hand, escapes the difficulty by an opposite course. He declines all inquiry into reality and causation, and maintains that the only office of philosophy is to observe and register the invariable relations of succession and similitude in phenomena. He does not necessarily deny the existence of God; but his personal belief, be it what it may, is a matter of utter indifference to his system. Religion and philosophy may perhaps go on side by side; but their provinces are wholly distinct, and therefore there is no need to attempt a reconciliation between them. God, as a first cause, lives like an Epicurean deity in undisturbed ease, apart from the world of phenomena, of which alone philosophy can take cognisance: philosophy, as the science of phenomena, contents itself with observing the actual state of things, without troubling itself to inquire how that state of things came into existence. Hence, neither Pantheism nor Positivism is troubled to explain the relation of the One to the Many; for the former acknowledges only the One, and the latter acknowledges only the Many.

It is between these two systems, both seductive from their apparent simplicity, and both simple only by mutilation, that the Philosophy of the Conditioned, of which Sir William Hamilton is the representative, endeavours to steer a middle course, at the risk of sharing the fate of most mediators in a quarrel,—being repudiated and denounced by both combatants, because it declares them to be both in the wrong. Against Pantheism, which is the natural development of the principle of Indifferentism, it enters a solemn protest, by asserting that the Absolute must be accepted in philosophy, not as a problem to be solved by reason, but as a reality to be believed in, though above reason; and that the pseudo-absolute, which Pantheism professes to exhibit in a positive conception, is shown, by the very fact of its being so conceived, not to be the true Absolute. Against Positivism, which is virtually Materialism, it protests no less strongly, maintaining that the philosophy which professes to explain the whole of nature by the aid of material laws alone, proceeds upon an assumption which does not merely dispense with God as a scientific hypothesis, but logically involves consequences which lead to a denial of His very existence. Between both extremes, it holds an intermediate position, neither aspiring, with Pantheism, to solve the problems of the Absolute, nor neglecting them, with Positivism, as altogether remote from the field of philosophical inquiry; but maintaining that such problems must necessarily arise, and must necessarily be taken into account in every adequate survey of human nature and human thought, and that philosophy, if it cannot solve them, is bound to show why they are insoluble.

Let us hear Hamilton's own words in relation to both the systems which he opposes. Against Pantheism, and the Philosophy of the Unconditioned in general, he says :—

"The Conditioned is the mean between two extremes, —two inconditionates, exclusive of each other, *neither of which can be conceived as possible,** but of which, on the

---

* It must be remembered that, to conceive a thing as possible, we must conceive the manner in which it is possible, but that we may believe in the fact without being able to conceive the manner.

principles of contradiction and excluded middle, *one must be admitted as necessary*. On this opinion, therefore, our faculties are shown to be weak, but not deceitful. The mind is not represented as conceiving two propositions, subversive of each other, as equally possible; but only as unable to understand as possible either of the two extremes; one of which, however, on the ground of their mutual repugnance, it is compelled to recognise as true. We are thus taught the salutary lesson, that the capacity of thought is not to be constituted into the measure of existence; and are warned from recognising the domain of our knowledge as necessarily co-extensive with the horizon of our faith. And by a wonderful revelation, we are thus, in the very consciousness of our inability to conceive aught above the relative and finite, inspired with a belief in the existence of something unconditioned beyond the sphere of all comprehensible reality."—*Discussions,* p. 15.

Against Materialism, and virtually against Positivism in general, he says :—

Had Hamilton distinctly expressed this, he might have avoided some very groundless criticisms, with which he has been assailed for maintaining a distinction between the provinces of conception and belief.

"If in man, intelligence be a free power,—in so far as its liberty extends, intelligence must be independent of necessity and matter; and a power independent of matter necessarily implies the existence of an immaterial subject —that is, a spirit. If, then, the original independence of intelligence on matter in the human constitution—in other words, if the spirituality of mind in man be supposed a datum of observation, in this datum is also given both the condition and the proof of a God. For we have only to infer, what analogy entitles us to do, that intelligence holds the same relative supremacy in the universe which it holds in us, and the first positive condition of a Deity is established, in the establishment of the absolute priority of a free creative intelligence. On the other hand, let us suppose the result of our study of man to be, that intelligence is only a product of matter, only a reflex of organization, such a doctrine would not only not afford no basis on which to rest any argument for a God, but, on the contrary, would positively warrant the atheist in denying His existence. For if, as the materialist maintains, the only intelligence of which we have any experience be a consequent of matter,—on this hypothesis, he not only cannot assume this order to be reversed in the relations of an intelligence beyond his observation, but, if he argue logically, he must positively conclude that, as in man, so in the universe, the phenomena of intelligence or design are only in their last analysis the products of a brute necessity. Psychological Materialism, if carried out fully and fairly to its conclusions, thus inevitably results in theological Atheism; as it has been well expressed by Dr. Henry More, *Nullus in microcosmo spiritus, nullus in macrocosmo Deus.* I do not, of course, mean to assert that all materialists deny or actually disbelieve a God. For, in very many cases, this would be at once an unmerited compliment to their reasoning, and an unmerited reproach to their faith."—*Lectures*, vol. i., p. 31.*

* This part of Hamilton's teaching is altogether repudiated by a recent writer, who, strangely enough, professes to be his disciple, while rejecting all that is really characteristic of his philosophy. Mr. Herbert Spencer, in his work on *First Principles*, endeavours to press Sir W. Hamilton into the service of Pantheism and Positivism together, by adopting the negative portion only of his philosophy—in which, in common with many other writers, he declares the absolute to be inconceivable by the mere intellect,—and rejecting the positive portions, in which he most emphatically maintains that the belief in a personal God is imperatively demanded by the facts of our moral and emotional consciousness. Mr. Spencer regards religion as nothing more than a consciousness of natural facts as being in their ultimate genesis unaccountable—a theory which is simply a combination of the positivist doctrine,

In the few places in which Hamilton speaks directly as a theologian, his language is in agreement with the general voice of

---

that we know only the relations of phenomena, with the pantheist assumption of the name of God to denote the substance or power which lies beyond phenomena. No theory can be more opposed to the philosophy of the conditioned than this. Sir W. Hamilton's fundamental principle is, that consciousness must be accepted entire, and that the moral and religious feelings, which are the primary source of our belief in a personal God, are in no way invalidated by the merely negative inferences which have deluded men into the assumption of an impersonal absolute; the latter not being legitimate deductions from consciousness rightly interpreted. Mr. Spencer, on the other hand, takes these negative inferences as the only basis of religion, and abandons Hamilton's great principle of the distinction between knowledge and belief, by quietly dropping out of his system the facts of consciousness which make such a distinction necessary. His whole system is, in fact, a pertinent illustration of Hamilton's remark, that "the phenomena of matter" [and of mind, he might add, treated by materialistic methods], "taken by themselves (you will observe the qualification, taken by themselves), so far from warranting any inference to the existence of a God, would, on the contrary, ground even an argument to his negation." Mr. Spencer, like Mr. Mill, denies the freedom of the will; and this, according to Hamilton, leads by logical consequence to Atheism.

Catholic theology down to the end of the seventeenth century, some specimens of which have been given on a previous page. Thus he says (*Discussions*, p. 15): "True, therefore, are the declarations of a pious philosophy,—'A God understood would be no God at all;' 'To think that God is, as we can think Him to be, is blasphemy.' The Divinity, in a certain sense, is revealed; in a certain sense is concealed: He is at once known and unknown. But the last and highest consecration of all true religion must be an altar Ἀγνώστῳ Θεῷ—'*To the unknown and unknowable God.*'" A little later (p. 20) he says: "We should not recoil to the opposite extreme; and though man be not identical with the Deity, still is he 'created in the image of God.' It is, indeed, only through an analogy of the human with the

Divine nature, that we are percipient and recipient of Divinity." In the first of these passages we have an echo of the language of Basil, the two Cyrils, and John Damascene, and of our own Hooker and Usher; while in the second we find the counter truth, intimated by Augustine and other Fathers,* and clearly stated by Aquinas, and which in the last century was elaborately expounded in the *Divine Analogy* of Bishop Browne,—namely, that though

---

* As *e.g.*, by Tertullian (*Adv. Marc.*, l. ii., c. 16): "Et hæc ergo imago censenda est Dei in homine, quod eosdem motus et sensus habeat humanus animus quos et Deus, licet non tales quales Deus: pro substantia enim, et status eorum et exitus distant." And by Gregory Nazianzen, Orat. xxxvii.: Ὠνομάσαμεν γὰρ ὡς ἡμῖν ἐφικτὸν ἐκ τῶν ἡμετέρων τὰ τοῦ Θεοῦ. And by Hilary, *De Trin.*, i. 19: "Comparatio enim terrenorum ad Deum nulla est; sed infirmitas nostræ intelligentiæ cogit species quasdam ex inferioribus, tanquam superiorum indices quærere; ut rerum familiarium consuetudine admovente, ex sensus nostri conscientia ad insoliti sensus opinionem educeremur."

we know not God in His own nature, yet are we not wholly ignorant of Him, but may attain to an imperfect knowledge of Him through the analogy between human things and Divine.

As regards theological results, therefore, there is nothing novel or peculiar in Hamilton's teaching; nor was he one who would have regarded novelty in theology as a recommendation. The peculiarity of his system, by which his reputation as a philosopher must ultimately stand or fall, is the manner in which he endeavoured to connect these theological conclusions with psychological principles; and thus to vindicate on philosophical grounds the position which Catholic divines had been compelled to take in the interests of dogmatic truth. That the absolute nature of God, as a supertemporal and yet personal Being, must be believed in as a fact, though inaccessible to reason as regards the manner of its possibility, is a position admitted, almost without exception, by divines who acknowledge the mystery of a personal Absolute—still more by those who acknowledge the yet deeper mystery of a Trinity in Unity. "We believe and know," says Bishop Sanderson of the mysteries of the Christian faith, "and that with fulness of assurance, that all these things are so as they are revealed in the Holy Scriptures, because the mouth of God, who is Truth itself, and cannot lie, hath spoken them; and our own reason upon this ground teacheth us to submit ourselves and it to *the obedience of faith,* for the τὸ ὅτι, that so it is. But then, for the τὸ πῶς, Nicodemus his question, *How can these things be?* it is no more possible for our weak understandings to comprehend that, than it is for the eyes of bats or owls to look steadfastly upon the body of the sun, when he shineth forth in his greatest strength."* This distinction Hamilton endeavoured to extend from the domain of Christian theology to that of philosophical speculation in general; to show that the unconditioned, as it is suggested in philosophy, no less than as it connects itself with revealed religion, is an object of belief, not of positive conception; and, consequently, that men cannot escape from mystery by rejecting revelation. " Above all," he says, " I am confirmed in my belief by the harmony between the doctrines of this philosophy, and those of revealed truth. . . . For this philosophy is professedly a scientific

* *Works*, vol. i., p. 233.

demonstration of the impossibility of that 'wisdom in high matters' which the Apostle prohibits us even to attempt; and it proposes, from the limitation of the human powers, from our impotence to comprehend what, however, we must admit, to show articulately why the 'secret things of God' cannot but be to man 'past finding out.'"* Faith in the inconceivable must thus become the ultimate refuge, even of the pantheist and the atheist, no less than of the Christian; the difference being, that while the last takes his stand on a faith which is in agreement alike with the authority of Scripture and the needs of human nature, the two former are driven to one which is equally opposed to both, as well as to the pretensions of their own philosophy.

* Discussions, p. 625.

The Philosophy of the Conditioned. 47

Deny the Trinity; deny the Personality of God: there yet remains that which no man can deny as the law of his own consciousness—*Time*. Conditioned existence is existence in time: to attain to a philosophy of the unconditioned, we must rise to the conception of existence out of time. The attempt may be made in two ways, and in two only. Either we may endeavour to conceive an absolutely first moment of time, beyond which is an existence having no duration and no succession; or we may endeavour to conceive time as an unlimited duration, containing an infinite series of successive antecedents and consequents, each conditioned in itself, but forming altogether an unconditioned whole. In other words, we may endeavour, with the Eleatics, to conceive pure existence apart and distinct from all phenomenal change; or we may endeavour, with Heraclitus, to conceive the universe as a system of incessant changes, immutable only in the law of its own mutability; for these two systems may be regarded as the type of all subsequent attempts. Both, however, alike aim at an object which is beyond positive conception, and which can be accepted only as something to be believed in spite of its inconceivability. To conceive an existence beyond the first moment of time, and to connect that existence as cause with the subsequent temporal succession of effects, we must conceive time itself as non-existent and then commencing to exist. But when we make the effort to conceive time as non-existent, we find it impossible to do so. Time, as the universal condition of human consciousness, clings round the very conception which strives to destroy it, clings round the language in which we speak of an existence *before* time. Nor are we more successful when we attempt to conceive an infinite regress of time, and an infinite series of dependent existences in time. To say nothing of the direct contradiction involved in the notion of an unconditioned *whole*,—a something completed,—composed of infinite parts—of parts never completed,—even if we abandon the Whole, and with it the Unconditioned, and attempt merely to conceive an infinite succession of conditioned existences —conditioned, absurdly enough, by nothing beyond themselves,—we find, that in order to do so, we must add moment to moment for ever—a process which would require an eternity for its accomplishment.* Moreover,

---

* See *Discussions*, p. 29. Of course by this is not meant that

the chain of dependent existences in this infinite succession is not, like a mathematical series, composed of abstract and homogeneous

no duration can be conceived except in a duration equally long—that a thousand years, *e. g.*, can only be conceived in a thousand years. A thousand years may be conceived as one unit: infinity cannot; for an unit is something complete, and therefore limited. What is meant is, that any period of time, however long, is conceived as capable of further increase, and therefore as not infinite. An infinite duration can have no time before or after it; and thus cannot resemble any portion of finite time, however great. When we dream of conceiving an infinite regress of time, says Sir W. Hamilton, "we only deceive ourselves by substituting the *indefinite* for the infinite, than which no two notions can be more opposed." This caution has not been attended to by some later critics. Thus, Dr. Whewell (*Philosophy of Discovery*, p. 324) says: "The definition of an infinite number is not that it contains all possible unities; but this—that the progress of numeration, being begun according to a certain law, goes on without limit." This is precisely Descartes' definition, not of the *infinite*, but of the *indefinite*. *Principia*, i. 26: "Nos autem illa omnia, in quibus sub aliqua consideratione nullum finem poterimus invenire, non quidem affirmabimus esse infinita, sed ut indefinita spectabimus." An indefinite time is that which is capable of perpetual addition: an infinite time is one so great as to admit of no addition. Surely "no two notions can be more opposed."

units; it is made up of divers phenomena, of a regressive line of causes, each distinct from the other. Wherever, therefore, I stop in my addition, I do not positively conceive the terms which lie beyond. I apprehend them only as a series of unknown *somethings*, of which I may believe *that* they are, but am unable to say *what* they are.

The cardinal point, then, of Sir W. Hamilton's philosophy, expressly announced as such by himself, is the absolute necessity, under any system of philosophy whatever, of acknowledging the existence of a sphere of belief beyond the limits of the sphere of thought. "The main scope of my speculation,"* he says, "is to show articulately that we *must believe*, as actual, much that we are unable (positively) *to conceive* as even pos-

* Letter to Mr. Calderwood. See *Lectures*, vol. ii., p. 534.

sible." It is, of course, beyond the range of such a speculation, by itself, to enter on an examination of the positive evidences in support of one form of belief rather than another. So far as it aims only at exhibiting an universal law of the human mind, it is of course compatible with all special forms of belief which do not contradict that law; and none, whatever their pretensions, can really contradict it. Hence the service which such a philosophy can render to the Christian religion must necessarily, from the nature of the case, be of an indirect and negative character. It prepares the way for a fair examination of the proper evidences of Christianity, by showing that there is no ground for any *à priori* prejudice against revelation, as appealing, for the acceptance of its highest truths, to faith rather than to reason; for that this appeal is common to all religions and to all philosophies, and cannot therefore be urged against one more than another. So far as certain difficulties are inherent in the constitution of the human mind itself, they must necessarily occupy the same position with respect to all religions alike. To exhibit the nature of these difficulties is a service to true religion; but it is the service of the pioneer, not of the builder; it does not prove the religion to be true; it only clears the ground for the production of the special evidences.

Where those evidences are to be found, Sir W. Hamilton has not failed to tell us. If mere intellectual speculations on the nature and origin of the material universe form a common ground in which the theist, the pantheist, and even the atheist, may alike expatiate, the moral and religious feelings of man—those facts of consciousness which have their direct source in the sense of personality and free will—plead with overwhelming evidence in behalf of a personal God, and of man's relation to Him, as a person to a person. We have seen, in a previous quotation, Hamilton's emphatic declaration that "psychological materialism, if carried out fully and fairly to its conclusions, inevitably results in theological atheism." In the same spirit he tells us that "it is only as man is a free intelligence, a moral power, that he is created after the image of God;"* that "with the proof of the moral nature of man, stands or falls the proof of the existence of a Deity;" that "the possibility of morality depends on the possibility of liberty;" that "if man be not a free agent, he is not the

* *Lectures*, vol. i., p. 30.

author of his actions, and has therefore no responsibility, no moral personality at all;"* and, finally, "that he who disbelieves the moral agency of man, must, in consistency with that opinion, disbelieve Christianity." † We have thus, in the positive and negative sides of this philosophy, both a reasonable ground of belief and a warning against presumption. By our immediate consciousness of a moral and personal nature, we are led to the belief in a moral and personal God : by our ignorance of the unconditioned, we are led to the further belief, that behind that moral and personal manifestation of God there lies concealed a mystery—the mystery of the Absolute and the Infinite; that our intellectual and moral qualities, though indi-

---

* *Lectures*, vol. i., p. 33.
† *Ibid.*, p. 42.

cating the nearest approach to the Divine Perfections which we are capable of conceiving, yet indicate them as analogous, not as identical; that we may naturally expect to find points where this analogy will fail us, where the function of the Infinite Moral Governor will be distinct from that of the finite moral servant; and where, consequently, we shall be liable to error in judging by human rules of the ways of God, whether manifested in nature or in revelation. Such is the true lesson to be learnt from a philosophy which tells us of a God who is "in a certain sense revealed, in a certain sense concealed—at once known and unknown."

It is not surprising that this philosophy, when compared with that of a critic like Mr. Mill, should stand out in clear and sharp antagonism. Mr. Mill is one of the most distinguished representatives of that school of Materialism which Sir W. Hamilton denounces as virtual Atheism. We do not mean that he consciously adopts the grosser tenets of the materialists. We are not aware that he has ever positively denied the existence of a soul distinct from the body, or maintained that the brain secretes thought as the liver secretes bile. But he is the advocate of a philosophical method which makes the belief in the existence of an immaterial principle superfluous and incongruous; he not only acknowledges no such distinction between the phenomena of mind and those of matter as to require the hypothesis of a free intelligence to account for it; he not only regards the ascertained laws of coexistence and succession in material phenomena as the type and rule according to which all phenomena whatever—those of internal consciousness no less than of external observation—are to be tested; but he even expressly denies the existence of that free will which Sir W. Hamilton regards as the indispensable condition of all morality and all religion.* Thus,

---

* That this is the real battle-ground between the two philosophers is virtually admitted by Mr. Mill himself at the end of his criticism. He says :—" The whole philosophy of Sir W. Hamilton seems to have had its character determined by the requirements of the doctrine of Free-will; and to that doctrine he clung, because he had persuaded himself that it afforded the only premises from which human reason could deduce the doctrines of natural religion. I believe that in this persuasion he was thoroughly his own dupe, and that his speculations have weakened the philosophical foundation of religion fully as much as they have confirmed it."—P. 549. Mr. Mill's whole philosophy, on the other hand, is determined by the requirements of the doctrine of Necessity; and to that doctrine he intrepidly adheres, in utter defiance of consciousness, and sometimes of his own consistency. Which of the two philosophers is really "his own dupe," Mr. Mill in believing that morality and religion can exist without free will—that a necessary agent can be responsible for his acts—or Sir W. Hamilton in maintaining the contrary, is a question which the former has by no means satisfactorily settled in his own favour.

The Philosophy of the Conditioned. 59

instead of recognising in the facts of intelligence "an order of existence diametrically in contrast to that displayed to us in the facts of the material universe,"* he regards both classes of facts as of the same kind, and explicable by the same laws; he abolishes the primary contrast of consciousness between the *ego* and the *non-ego*—the person and the thing; he reduces man to a thing, instead of a person,—to one among the many phenomena of the universe, determined by the same laws of invariable antecedence and consequence, included under the same formulæ of empirical generalization. He thus makes man the slave, and not the master of nature; passively carried along in the current of successive phenomena; unable, by any act of free will, to arrest a single wave in its

* Hamilton, *Lectures*, vol. i., p. 29.

course, or to divert it from its ordained direction.

This diametrical antagonism between the two philosophers is not limited to their first principles, but extends, as might naturally be expected, to every subordinate science of which the immediate object is mental, and not material. Logic, instead of being, as Sir W. Hamilton regards it, an *à priori* science of the necessary laws of thought, is with Mr. Mill a science of observation, investigating those operations of the understanding which are subservient to the estimation of evidence.* The axioms of Mathematics, which the former philosopher regards, with Kant, as necessary thoughts, based on the *à priori* intuitions of space and time, the latter† declares to be "experimental

---

* Mill's *Logic.* Introduction, § 7.   † *Ibid.*, book ii. 5, § 4.

truths; generalizations from observation." Psychology, which with Hamilton is especially the philosophy of man as a free and personal agent, is with Mill the science of "the uniformities of succession; the laws, whether ultimate or derivative, according to which one mental state succeeds another."* And finally, in the place of Ethics, as the science of the *à priori* laws of man's moral obligations, we are presented, in Mr. Mill's system, with Ethology, the "science which determines the kind of character produced, in conformity to the general laws of mind, by any set of circumstances, physical and moral." †

The contrast between the two philosophers being thus thoroughgoing, it was natural to expect beforehand that an *Examination of*

* Mill's *Logic*, book vi. 4, § 3. † *Ibid.*, book vi. 5, § 4.

Sir William Hamilton's Philosophy, by Mr. Mill, would contain a sharp and vigorous assault on the principal doctrines of that philosophy. And this expectation has been amply fulfilled. But there was also reason to expect, from the ability and critical power displayed in Mr. Mill's previous writings, that his assault, whether successful or not in overthrowing his enemy, would at least be guided by a clear knowledge of that enemy's position and purposes; that his dissent would be accompanied by an intelligent apprehension, and an accurate statement, of the doctrines dissented from. In this expectation, we regret to say, we have been disappointed. Not only is Mr. Mill's attack on Hamilton's philosophy, with the exception of some minor details, unsuccessful; but we are compelled to add, that with regard to the three fundamental doctrines of that philosophy—the Relativity of Knowledge, the Incognisability of the Absolute and Infinite, and the distinction between Reason and Faith—Mr. Mill has, throughout his criticism, altogether missed the meaning of the theories he is attempting to assail.

This is a serious charge to bring against a writer of such eminence as Mr. Mill, and one which should not be advanced without ample proof. First, then, of the Relativity of Knowledge.

The assertion that all our knowledge is relative,—in other words, that we know things only under such conditions as the laws of our cognitive faculties impose upon us,—is a statement which looks at first sight like a truism, but which really contains an answer to a very important question,—Have we reason to believe that the laws of our cognitive faculties impose any conditions at all?—that the mind in any way reacts on the objects affecting it, so as to produce a result different from that which would be produced were it merely a passive recipient? "The mind of man," says Bacon, "is far from the nature of a clear and equal glass, wherein the beams of things shall reflect according to their true incidence; nay, it is rather like an enchanted glass, full of superstition and imposture, if it be not delivered and reduced." Can what Bacon says of the fallacies of the mind be also said of its proper cognitions? Does the mind, by its own action, in any way distort the appearance of the things presented to it; and if so, how far does the distortion extend, and in what manner is it to be rectified? To trace the course

The Philosophy of the Conditioned. 65

of this inquiry, from the day when Plato compared the objects perceived by the senses to the shadows thrown by fire on the wall of a cave, to the day when Kant declared that we know only phenomena, not things in themselves, would be to write the history of philosophy. We can only at present call attention to one movement in that history, which was, in effect, a revolution in philosophy. The older philosophers in general distinguished between the senses and the intellect, regarding the former as deceptive and concerned with phenomena alone, the latter as trustworthy and conversant with the realities of things. Hence arose the distinction between the sensible and the intelligible world—between things as perceived by sense and things as apprehended by intellect—between Phenomenology and

Ontology. Kant rejected this distinction, holding that the intellect, as well as the sense, imposes its own forms on the things presented to it, and is therefore cognisant only of phenomena, not of things in themselves. The logical result of this position would be the abolition of ontology as a science of things in themselves, and, *à fortiori*, of that highest branch of ontology which aims at a knowledge of the Absolute* κατ' ἐξοχήν, of the unconditioned first principle of all things. If the mind, in every act of thought, imposes its own forms on its objects, to think

---

* The term *absolute*, in the sense of *free from relation*, may be used in two applications;—1st, To denote the nature of a thing as it is in itself, as distinguished from its appearance to us. Here it is used only in a subordinate sense, as meaning out of relation to human knowledge. 2ndly, To denote the nature of a thing as independent of all other things, as having no relation to any other thing as the condition of its existence. Here it is used in its highest sense, as meaning out of relation to anything else.

The Philosophy of the Conditioned. 67

is to condition, and the unconditioned is the unthinkable. Such was the logical result of Kant's principles, but not the actual result. For Kant, by distinguishing between the Understanding and the Reason, and giving to the latter an indirect yet positive cognition of the Unconditioned as a regulative principle of thought, prepared the way for the systems of Schelling and Hegel, in which this indirect cognition is converted into a direct one, by investing the reason, thus distinguished as the special faculty of the unconditioned, with a power of intuition emancipated from the conditions of space and time, and even of subject and object, or a power of thought emancipated from the laws of identity and contradiction.

The theory of Hamilton is a modification ✓ of that of Kant, intended to obviate these consequences, and to relieve the Kantian doctrine itself from the inconsistency which gave rise to them. So long as the reason is regarded as a separate faculty from the understanding, and things in themselves as ideas of the reason, so long the apparent contradictions, which encumber the attempt to conceive the unconditioned, must be regarded as inherent in the constitution of the reason itself, and as the result of its legitimate exercise on its proper objects. This sceptical conclusion Hamilton endeavoured to avoid by rejecting the distinction between the understanding and the reason as separate faculties, regarding the one as the legitimate and positive, the other as the illegitimate and negative, exercise of one and the same faculty. He thus announces, in opposition to Kant, the fundamental doctrine of the

Conditioned, as "the distinction between intelligence *within* its legitimate sphere of operation, impeccable, and intelligence *beyond* that sphere, affording (by abuse) the occasions of error."* Hamilton, like Kant, maintained that all our cognitions are compounded of two elements, one contributed by the object known, and the other by the mind knowing. But the very conception of a relation implies the existence of things to be related; and the knowledge of an object, as in relation to our mind, necessarily implies its existence out of that relation. But as so existing, it is unknown: we believe *that* it is; we know not *what* it is. How far it resembles, or how far it does not resemble, the object apprehended by us, we cannot say, for we have no means of comparing the two together.

* *Discussions*, p. 633.

Instead, therefore, of saying with Kant, that reason is subject to an inevitable delusion, by which it mistakes the regulative principles of its own thoughts for the representations of real things, Hamilton would say that the reason, while compelled to believe in the existence of these real things, is not legitimately entitled to make any positive representation of them as of such or such a nature; and that the contradictions into which it falls when attempting to do so are due to an illegitimate attempt to transcend the proper boundaries of positive thought.

This theory does not, in itself, contain any statement of the mode in which we perceive the material world, whether directly by presentation, or indirectly by representative images; and perhaps it might, without any great violence, be adapted to more than one of the current hypotheses on this point. But that to which it most easily adjusts itself is that maintained by Hamilton himself under the name of *Natural Realism*. To speak of perception as a *relation* between mind and matter, naturally implies the presence of both correlatives; though each may be modified by its contact with the other. The acid may act on the alkali, and the alkali on the acid, in forming the neutral salt; but each of the ingredients is as truly present as the other, though each enters into the compound in a modified form. And this is equally the case in perception, even if we suppose various media to intervene between the ultimate object and the perceiving mind,—such, *e. g.*, as the rays of light and the sensitive organism in vision,— so long as these media are material, like the ultimate object itself.

Whether the object, properly so called, in vision, be the rays of light in contact with the organ, or the body emitting or reflecting those rays, is indifferent to the present question, so long as a material object of some kind or other is supposed to be perceived, and not merely an inmaterial representation of such an object. To speak of our perceptions as mere modifications of mind produced by an unknown cause, would be like maintaining that the acid is modified by the influence of the alkali without entering into combination with it. Such a view might perhaps be tolerated, in connection with the theory of relativity, by an indulgent interpretation of language, but it is certainly not that which the language of the theory most naturally suggests.

All this Mr. Mill entirely misapprehends.

The Philosophy of the Conditioned. 73

He quotes a passage from Hamilton's Lectures, in which the above theory of Relativity is clearly stated as the mean between the extremes of Idealism and Materialism, and then proceeds to comment as follows :—

"The proposition, that our cognitions of objects are only in part dependent on the objects themselves, and in part on elements superadded by our organs or our minds, is not identical, nor *prima facie* absurd. It cannot, however, warrant the assertion that all our knowledge, but only that the part so added, is relative. If our author had gone as far as Kant, and had said that all which constitutes knowledge is put in by the mind itself, he would have really held, in one of its forms, the doctrine of the relativity of our knowledge. But what he does say, far from implying that the whole of our knowledge is relative, distinctly imports that all of it which is real and authentic is the reverse. If any part of what we fancy that we perceive in the objects themselves, originates in the perceiving organs or in the cognising mind, thus much is purely relative; but since, by supposition, it does not all so originate, the part that does not is as much absolute as if it were not liable to be mixed up with these delusive subjective impressions."—(P. 30.)

Mr. Mill, therefore, supposes that *wholly relative* must mean *wholly mental;* in other words, that to say that a thing is wholly due to a relation between mind and matter is equivalent to saying that it is wholly due to mind alone. On the contrary, we maintain that Sir W. Hamilton's language is far more accurate than Mr. Mill's, and that the above theory can with perfect correctness be described as one of *total relativity;* and this from two points of view. First, as opposed to the theory of partial relativity generally held by the pre-Kantian philosophers, according to which our sensitive cognitions are relative, our intellectual ones absolute. Secondly, as asserting that the object of perception, though composed of elements partly material, partly mental, yet exhibits both alike in a form modified by their relation to each other. The composition is not a mere mechanical juxtaposition, in which each part, though acting on the other, retains its own characteristics unchanged. It may be rather likened to a chemical fusion, in which both elements are present, but each of them is affected by the composition. The material part, therefore, is not "as much absolute as if it were not liable to be mixed up with subjective impressions."

But we must hear the continuation of Mr. Mill's criticism :—

"The admixture of the relative element not only does not take away the absolute character of the remainder, but does not even (if our author is right) prevent us from recognising it. The confusion, according to him, is not inextricable. It is for us to 'analyse and distinguish what elements' in an 'act of knowledge' are contributed by the object, and what by our organs, or by the mind. We may neglect to do this, and as far as the mind's share is concerned, we can only do it by the help of philosophy; but it is a task to which, in his opinion, philosophy is equal. By thus stripping off such of the elements in our apparent cognitions of things as are but cognitions of something in us, and consequently relative, we may succeed in uncovering the pure nucleus, the direct intuitions of things in themselves; as we correct the observed positions of the heavenly bodies by allowing for the error due to the refracting influence of the atmospheric medium, an influence which does not alter the facts, but only our perception of them."

Surely Mr. Mill here demands much more of philosophy than Sir W. Hamilton deems it capable of accomplishing. Why may not Hamilton, like Kant, distinguish between the permanent and necessary, and the variable and contingent—in other words, between the subjective and the objective elements of consciousness, without therefore obtaining a "direct intuition of things in themselves?" Why may he not distinguish between space and time as the forms of our sensitive cognitions, and the things perceived in space and time, which constitute the matter of the same cognitions, without thereby having an intuition, on the one hand, of pure space and time with nothing in them, or on the other, of things in themselves out of space and time? If certain elements are always present in perception, while certain others change with every act, I may surely infer that the one is due to the permanent subject, the other to the variable object, without thereby knowing what each would be if it could be discerned apart from the other. "A direct intuition of things in themselves," according to Kant and Hamilton, is an intuition of things out of space and time. Does Mr. Mill suppose that any natural Realist professes to have such an intuition?

The same error of supposing that a doctrine of relativity is necessarily a doctrine of Idealism, that "matter known only in relation to us" can mean nothing more than "matter known only through the mental impressions of which it is the unknown cause,"* runs through the whole of Mr. Mill's argument against this portion of Sir W. Hamilton's teaching. That argument, though repeated in various forms, may be briefly summed up

* The assumption that these two expressions are or ought to be synonymous is tacitly made by Mr. Mill at the opening of this chapter. He opens it with a passage from the *Discussions*, in which Hamilton says that the existence of *things in themselves* is only indirectly revealed to us "through certain qualities *related to our faculties of knowledge;*" and then proceeds to show that the author did not hold the doctrine which these phrases "seem to convey in the only substantial meaning capable of being attached to them;" namely, "that we know nothing of *objects* except their

The Philosophy of the Conditioned.

in one thesis ; namely, that the doctrine that our knowledge of matter is wholly relative is incompatible with the distinction, which Hamilton expressly makes, between the primary and secondary qualities of body.

The most curious circumstance about this criticism is, that, if not directly borrowed from, it has at least been carefully anticipated by, Hamilton himself. Of the distinction between primary and secondary qualities, as acknowledged by Descartes and Locke,

---

existence, and the impressions produced by them upon the human mind." Having thus quietly assumed that "things in themselves" are identical with "objects," and "relations" with "impressions on the human mind," Mr. Mill bases his whole criticism on this tacit *petitio principii.* He is not aware that though Reid sometimes uses the term *relative* in this inaccurate sense, Hamilton expressly points out the inaccuracy and explains the proper sense.— (See *Reid's Works,* pp. 313, 322.)

whose theory of external perception is identical with that which Mr. Mill would force on Hamilton himself, Hamilton says : "On the general doctrine, however, of these philosophers, both classes of qualities, as known, are confessedly only states of our own minds; and while we have no right from a subjective affection to infer the existence, far less the corresponding character of the existence, of any objective reality, it is evident that their doctrine, if fairly evolved, would result in a dogmatic or in a sceptical negation of the primary no less than of the secondary qualities of body, as more than appearances in and for us."* It is astonishing that Mr. Mill, who pounces eagerly on every imaginable instance of Hamilton's inconsistency, should have neglected to notice this, which, if his

---

* *Reid's Works*, p. 840.

criticism be true, is the most glaring inconsistency of all.

But Hamilton continues : " It is therefore manifest that the fundamental position of a consistent theory of dualistic realism is—that our cognitions of Extension and its modes are not wholly ideal—that although Space be a native, necessary, *à priori* form of imagination, and so far, therefore, a mere subjective state, that there is, at the same time, competent to us, in an *immediate* perception of external things, the *consciousness* of a really existent, of a really objective, *extended* world." Here we have enunciated in one breath, first the subjectivity of space, which is the logical basis of the relative theory of perception; and secondly, the objectivity of the extended world, which is the logical basis of the distinction between primary and secondary qualities. It is manifest, therefore, that Hamilton had not, as Mr. Mill supposes, ceased to hold the one theory when he adopted the other.*

The key to all this is not difficult to find. It is simply that *objective existence* does not mean existence *per se;* and that a *phenomenon* does not mean a mere mode of mind. Objective existence is existence *as an object*, in perception, and therefore in relation ; and a phenomenon may be material, as well as mental. The thing *per se* may be only the unknown cause of what we directly know ; but what we directly know is something more than our own sensations. In other words, the phenomenal effect is material as well as the cause, and is, indeed, that from which our primary conceptions of matter are

* See *Examination,* p. 28.

derived. Matter does not cease to be matter when modified by its contact with mind, as iron does not cease to be iron when smelted and forged. A horseshoe is something very different from a piece of iron ore; and a man may be acquainted with the former without ever having seen the latter, or knowing what it is like. But would Mr. Mill therefore say that the horseshoe is merely a subjective affection of the skill of the smith—that it is not iron modified by the workman, but the workman or his art impressed by iron?

If, indeed, Hamilton had said with Locke, that the primary qualities are in the bodies themselves, whether we perceive them or no,* he would have laid himself open to Mr. Mill's criticism. But he expressly rejects this statement, and contrasts it with the

* *Essay*, ii. 8, § 23.

more cautious language of Descartes, "ut sunt, vel saltem esse possunt."* The secondary qualities are mere affections of consciousness, which cannot be conceived as existing except in a conscious subject. The primary qualities are qualities of body, as perceived in relation to the percipient mind, *i. e.*, of the phenomenal body perceived as in space. How far they exist in the real body out of relation to us, Hamilton does not attempt to decide.† They are inseparable from our

---

* *Reid's Works*, p. 839.

† We have been content to argue this question, as Mr. Mill himself argues it, on the supposition that Sir W. Hamilton held that we are directly percipient of primary qualities in external bodies. Strictly speaking, however, Hamilton held that the primary qualities are immediately perceived only in our organism as extended, and inferred to exist in extra-organic bodies. The external world is immediately apprehended only in its secundo-primary character, as resisting our locomotive energy. But as the organism, in this theory, is a material *non-ego* equally with the rest of matter, and as to press this distinction would only affect the

conception of body, which is derived exclusively from the phenomenon ; they may or may not be separable from the thing as it is in itself.

Under this explanation, it is manifest that the doctrine, that matter as a subject or substratum of attributes is unknown and unknowable, is totally different from that of cosmothetic idealism, with which Mr Mill

---

verbal accuracy, not the substantial justice, of Mr. Mill's criticisms, we have preferred to meet him on the ground he has himself chosen. The same error, of supposing that "presentationism" is identical with "noumenalism," and "phenomenalism" with "representationism," runs through the whole of Mr. Stirling's recent criticism of Hamilton's theory of perception. It is curious, however, that the very passage (*Lectures*, i., p. 146) which Mr. Mill cites as proving that Hamilton, in spite of his professed phenomenalism, was an unconscious noumenalist, is employed by Mr. Stirling to prove that, in spite of his professed presentationism, he was an unconscious representationist. The two critics tilt at Hamilton from opposite quarters : he has only to stand aside and let them run against each other.

confounds it;* and that a philosopher may without inconsistency accept the former and reject the latter. The former, while it holds the material substance to be unknown, does not deny that some of the attributes of matter are perceived immediately as material, though, it may be, modified by contact with mind. The latter maintains that the attributes, as well as the substance, are not perceived immediately as material, but mediately through the intervention of immaterial representatives. It is also manifest that, in answer to Mr. Mill's question, which of Hamilton's two "cardinal doctrines," Relativity or Natural Realism, " is to be taken in a non-natural sense,"† we must say, neither. The two doctrines are quite compatible with each other, and neither requires a non-natural

---

* *Examination*, p. 23. † *Examination*, p. 20.

The Philosophy of the Conditioned. 87

interpretation to reconcile it to its companion.

The doctrine of relativity derives its chief practical value from its connection with the next great doctrine of Hamilton's philosophy, the incognisability of the Absolute and the Infinite. For this doctrine brings Ontology into contact with Theology; and it is only in relation to theology that ontology acquires a practical importance. With respect to the other two "ideas of the pure reason," as Kant calls them, the human soul and the world, the question, whether we know them as realities or as phenomena, may assist us in dealing with certain metaphysical difficulties, but need not affect our practical conduct. For we have an immediate intuition of the attributes of mind and matter, at least as phenomenal objects, and by these intuitions may be tested the accuracy of the conceptions derived from them, sufficiently for all practical purposes. A man will equally avoid walking over a precipice, and is logically as consistent in avoiding it, whether he regard the precipice as a real thing, or as a mere phenomenon. But in the province of theology this is not the case. We have no immediate intuition of the Divine attributes, even as phenomena; we only infer their existence and nature from certain similar attributes of which we are immediately conscious in ourselves. And hence arises the question, How far does the similarity extend, and to what extent is the accuracy of our conceptions guaranteed by the intuition, not of the object to be conceived, but of something more or less nearly resembling it? But this is not all. Our knowledge of God, originally derived from personal consciousness, receives accession from two other sources—from the external world, as His work; and from revelation, as His word; and the conclusions derived from each have to be compared together. Should any discrepancy arise between them, are we at once warranted in rejecting one class of conclusions in favour of the other two, or two in favour of the third? or are we at liberty to say that our knowledge in respect of all alike is of such an imperfect and indirect character that we are warranted in believing that some reconciliation may exist, though our ignorance prevents us from discovering what it is? Here at least is a practical question of the very highest importance. In the early part of our previous remarks, we have endeavoured to show how this question has been answered by orthodox theologians of various ages, and how Sir W. Hamilton's philosophy supports that answer. We have now to consider Mr Mill's chapter of criticisms.

It is always unfortunate to make a stumble on the threshold; and Mr. Mill's opening paragraph makes two. "The name of God," he says, "is veiled under two extremely abstract phrases, 'the Infinite and the Absolute.' . . . But it is one of the most unquestionable of all logical maxims, that the meaning of the abstract must be sought in the concrete, and not conversely."*—Now, in the first place, "the Infinite" and "the Absolute," even in the sense in which they are both predicable of God, are no more names of God than "the creature" and "the finite" are names of man. They are the

* *Examination*, p. 32.

names of certain attributes, which further inquiry may, perhaps, show to belong to God and to no other being, but which do not in their signification express this, and do not constitute our primary idea of God, which is that of a Person. Men may believe in an absolute and infinite, without in any proper sense believing in God ; and thousands upon thousands of pious men have prayed to a personal God, who have never heard of the absolute and the infinite, and who would not understand the expressions if they heard them. But, in the second place, " the absolute" and "the infinite," in Sir W. Hamilton's sense of the terms, cannot both be names of God, for the simple reason that they are contradictory of each other, and are proposed as alternatives which cannot both be accepted as predicates of the same subject. For Hamilton, whatever Mr. Mill may do, did not fall into the absurdity of maintaining that God in some of His attributes is absolute without being infinite, and in others is infinite without being absolute.*

But we have not yet done with this single paragraph. After thus making two errors in his exposition of his opponent's doctrine, Mr. Mill immediately proceeds to a third, in his criticism of it. By following his "most unquestionable of all logical maxims," and substituting the name of God in the place of "the Infinite" and "the Absolute," he exactly reverses Sir W. Hamilton's argument, and makes his own attempted refutation of it a glaring *ignoratio elenchi*.

One of the purposes of Hamilton's argument is to show that we have no positive

---

* See *Examination*, p. 35.

The Philosophy of the Conditioned.

conception of an Infinite Being; that when we attempt to form such a conception, we do but produce a distorted representation of the finite; and hence, that our so-called conception of the infinite is not the true infinite. Hence it is not to be wondered at—nay, it is a natural consequence of this doctrine,—that our positive conception of God as a Person cannot be included under this pseudo-concept of the Infinite. Whereas Mr. Mill, by laying down the maxim that the meaning of the abstract must be sought in the concrete, quietly assumes that this pseudo-infinite is a proper predicate of God, to be tested by its applicability to the subject, and that what Hamilton says of *this* infinite cannot be true unless it is also true of God. Of this refutation, Hamilton, were he living, might truly say, as he said of a former criticism on another part of his writings,—" This elaborate parade of argument is literally answered in two words—*Quis dubitavit?*"

But if the substitution of God for the Infinite be thus a perversion of Hamilton's argument, what shall we say to a similar substitution in the case of the Absolute? Hamilton distinctly tells us that there is one sense of the term *absolute* in which it is contradictory of the infinite, and therefore is not predicable of God at all. Mr. Mill admits that Hamilton, throughout the greater part of his arguments, employs the term in this sense; and he then actually proceeds to "test" these arguments "by substituting the concrete, God, for the abstract, Absolute;" *i.e.*, by substituting God for something which Hamilton defines as contradictory to the nature of God. Can the force of confusion go further? Is it possible for perverse criticism more utterly, we do not say to misrepresent, but literally to invert an author's meaning?

The source of all these errors, and of a great many more, is simply this. Mr. Mill is aware, from Hamilton's express assertion, that the word *absolute* may be used in two distinct and even contradictory senses; but he is wholly unable to see what those senses are, or when Hamilton is using the term in the one sense, and when in the other. Let us endeavour to clear up some of this confusion.

Hamilton's article on the Philosophy of the Unconditioned is a criticism, partly of Schelling, partly of Cousin; and Schelling and Cousin only attempted in a new form, under the influence of the Kantian philosophy, to solve the problem with which philosophy in all ages has attempted to grapple,—the problem of the Unconditioned.

"The unconditioned" is a term which, while retaining the same general meaning, admits of various applications, particular or universal. It may be the unconditioned as regards some special relation, or the unconditioned as regards all relations whatever. Thus there may be the unconditioned in Psychology—the human soul considered as a substance; the unconditioned in Cosmology —the world considered as a single whole; the unconditioned in Theology—God in His own nature, as distinguished from His manifestations to us; or, finally, the unconditioned *par excellence*—the unconditioned in Ontology—the being on which all other being depends. It is of course possible to identify any one of the three first with the last. It

The Philosophy of the Conditioned. 97

is possible to adopt a system of Egoism, and to maintain that all phenomena are modes of my mind, and that the substance of my mind is the only real existence. It is possible to adopt a system of Materialism, and to maintain that all phenomena are modes of matter, and that the material substance of the world is the only real existence. Or it is possible to adopt a system of Pantheism, and to maintain that all phenomena are modes of the Divine existence, and that God is the only reality. But the several notions are in themselves distinct, though one may ultimately be predicated of another.

The general notion of the Unconditioned is the same in all these cases, and all must finally culminate in the last, the Unconditioned *par excellence*. The general notion is that of the One as distinguished from the

Many, the substance from its accidents, the permanent reality from its variable modifications. Thought, will, sensation, are modes of my existence. What is the *I* that is one and the same in all? Extension, figure, resistance, are attributes of matter. What is the one substance to which these attributes belong? But the generalisation cannot stop here. If matter differs from mind, the *non-ego* from the *ego*, as one thing from another, there must be some special point of difference, which is the condition of the existence of each in this or that particular manner. Unconditioned existence, therefore, in the highest sense of the term, cannot be the existence of *this* as distinguished from *that*; it must be existence *per se*, the ground and principle of all conditioned or special existence. This is the Unconditioned, properly so called : the unconditioned in Schelling's sense, as the indifference of subject and object : and it is against this that Hamilton's arguments are directed.

The question is this. Is this Unconditioned a mere abstraction, the product of our own minds ; or can it be conceived as having a real existence *per se*, and, as such, can it be identified with God as the source of all existence ? Hamilton maintains that it is a mere abstraction, and cannot be so identified ; that, far from being " a name of God," it is a name of nothing at all. " By abstraction," he says, " we annihilate the object, and by abstraction we annihilate the subject of consciousness. But what remains ? *Nothing.*" When we attempt to conceive it as a reality, we " hypostatise the zero."*

---

* *Discussions*, p. 21.

In order to conceive the Unconditioned existing as a thing, we must conceive it as existing out of relation to everything else. For if nothing beyond itself is necessary as a condition of its existence, it can exist separate from everything else; and its pure existence as the unconditioned is so separate. It must therefore be conceivable as the sole existence, having no plurality beyond itself; and as simple, having no plurality within itself. For if we cannot conceive it as existing apart from other things, we cannot conceive it as independent of them; and if we conceive it as a compound of parts, we have further to ask as before, what is the principle of unity which binds these parts into one whole? If there is such a principle, this is the true unconditioned; if there is no such principle, there is no unconditioned; for that which cannot exist except as a compound is dependent for its existence on that of its several constituents. The unconditioned must therefore be conceived as one, as simple, and as universal.

Is such a conception possible, whether in ordinary consciousness, as Cousin says, or in an extraordinary intuition, as Schelling says? Let us try the former. Consciousness is subject to the law of Time. A phenomenon is presented to us in time, as dependent on some previous phenomenon or thing. I wish to pursue the chain in thought till I arrive at something independent. If I could reach in thought a beginning of time, and discover some first fact with nothing preceding it, I should conceive time as absolute—as completed,—and the unconditioned as the first thing in time, and therefore as completed also, for it may be considered by itself, apart from what depends upon it. Or if time be considered as having no beginning, thought would still be able to represent to itself that infinity, could it follow out the series of antecedents for ever. But is either of these alternatives possible to thought? If not, we must confess that the unconditioned is inconceivable by ordinary consciousness; and we must found philosophy, with Schelling, on the annihilation of consciousness.

But though Hamilton himself distinguishes between the *unconditioned* and the *absolute*, using the former term generally, for that which is out of all relation, and the latter specially, for that which is out of all relation as complete and finished, his opponent Cousin uses the latter term in a wider sense, as synonymous with the former, and the *infinite* as coextensive with both. This, however, does not affect the validity of Hamilton's argument. For if it can be shown that the absolute and the infinite (in Hamilton's sense) are both inconceivable, the unconditioned (or absolute in Cousin's sense), which must be conceived as one or the other, is inconceivable also. Or, conversely, if it can be shown that the unconditioned, the unrelated in general, is inconceivable, it follows that the absolute and the infinite, as both involving the unrelated, are inconceivable also.

We may now proceed with Mr. Mill's criticism. He says :—

"Absolute, in the sense in which it stands related to Infinite, means (conformably to its etymology) that which is finished or completed. There are some things of which the utmost ideal amount is a limited quantity, though a quantity never actually reached. . . We may speak of absolutely, but not of infinitely, pure water. The purity of water is not a fact of which, whatever degree we suppose attained, there remains a greater beyond. It has an absolute limit: it is capable of being finished or complete, in thought, if not in reality."—(P. 34.)

This criticism is either incorrect or *nihil ad rem*. If meant as a statement of Hamilton's use of the term, it is incorrect: *absolute*, in Hamilton's philosophy, does not mean simply "completed," but "out of relation as completed;" *i.e.*, self-existent in its completeness, and not implying the existence of anything else. If meant in any other sense than Hamilton's, it is irrelevant. Can Mr. Mill really have believed that Schelling thought it necessary to invent an intellectual intuition out of time and out of consciousness, in order to contemplate "an ideal limited quantity," such as the complete purity of water?

Mr. Mill continues :—

"Though the idea of Absolute is thus contrasted with that of Infinite, the one is equally fitted with the other to be predicated of God; but not in respect of the same attributes. There is no incorrectness of speech in the phrase Infinite Power: because the notion it expresses is that of a Being who has the power of doing all things which we know or can conceive, and more. But in speaking of knowledge, Absolute is the proper word, and not Infinite. The highest degree of knowledge that can be spoken of with a meaning, only amounts to knowing all that there is to be known: when that point is reached, knowledge has attained its utmost limit. So of goodness or justice: they cannot be more than perfect. There are not infinite degrees of right. The will is either entirely right, or wrong in different degrees."—(P. 35.)

Surely, whatever Divine power can do, Divine knowledge can know as possible to be done. The one, therefore, must be as infinite as the other. And what of Divine goodness? An angel or a glorified saint is absolutely good in Mr. Mill's sense of the term. His "will is entirely right." Does Mr. Mill mean to say that there is no difference, even in degree, between the goodness of God and that of one of His creatures? But, even supposing his statement to be true, how is it relevant to the matter under discussion? Can Mr. Mill possibly be ignorant that all these attributes are relations; that the Absolute in Hamilton's sense, "the unconditionally limited," is not predicable of God at all; and that when divines and philosophers speak of the absolute nature of God, they mean a nature in which there is no distinction of attributes at all?

Mr. Mill then proceeds to give a summary of Hamilton's arguments against Cousin, preparatory to refuting them. In the course of this summary he says:—

"Let me ask, *en passant*, where is the necessity for

supposing that, if the Absolute, or, to speak plainly, if God, is only known to us in the character of a cause, he must therefore 'exist merely as a cause,' and be merely 'a mean towards an end?' It is surely possible to maintain that the Deity is known to us only as he who feeds the ravens, without supposing that the Divine Intelligence exists solely in order that the ravens may be fed."*—(P. 42.)

On this we would remark, *en passant*, that this is precisely Hamilton's own doctrine, that the sphere of our belief is more ex-

* In a note to this passage, Mr. Mill makes some sarcastic comments on an argument of Hamilton's against Cousin's theory that God is necessarily determined to create. "On this hypothesis," says Hamilton, "God, as necessarily determined to pass from absolute essence to relative manifestation, is determined to pass either from the better to the worse, or from the worse to the better." Mr. Mill calls this argument "a curiosity of dialectics," and answers, "Perfect wisdom would have begun to will the new state at the precise moment when it began to be better than the old." Hamilton is not speaking of states of things, but of states of the Divine nature, as creative or not creative; and Mr. Mill's argument, to refute Hamilton, must suppose a time when the new nature of God begins to be better than the old! Mr. Mill would perhaps have spoken of Hamilton's argument with more respect had he known that it is taken from Plato.

tensive than that of our knowledge. The purport of Hamilton's argument is to show that the Absolute, as conceived by Cousin, is not a true Absolute (*Infinito-Absolute*), and therefore does not represent the real nature of God. His argument is this: "Cousin's Absolute exists merely as a cause: God does not exist merely as a cause: therefore Cousin's Absolute is not God." Mr. Mill actually mistakes the position which Hamilton is opposing for that which he is maintaining. Such an error does not lead us to expect much from his subsequent refutation.

His first criticism is a curious specimen of his reading in philosophy. He says:—

"When the True or the Beautiful are spoken of, the phrase is meant to include all things whatever that are true, or all things whatever that are beautiful. If this rule is good for other abstractions, it is good for the Absolute. The word is devoid of meaning unless in reference to predicates of some sort. . . . If we are told, therefore, that there is some Being who is, or which is, the Absolute,—not something absolute, but the Absolute itself,—the proposition can be understood in no other sense than that the supposed Being possesses in absolute completeness *all* predicates; is absolutely good and absolutely bad; absolutely wise and absolutely stupid; and so forth."*—(P. 43.)

Plato expressly distinguishes between "the beautiful" and "things that are beautiful," as the One in contrast to the Many—the Real in contrast to the Apparent.† It is, of course, quite possible that Plato may be

---

* In support of this position, Mr. Mill cites Hegel—" What kind of an absolute Being is that which does not contain in itself all that is actual, even evil included?" We are not concerned to defend Hegel's position; but he was not quite so absurd as to mean what Mr. Mill supposes him to have meant. Does not Mr. Mill know that it was one of Hegel's fundamental positions, that the Divine nature cannot be expressed by a plurality of predicates?

† *Republic*, book v., p. 479.

wrong, and Mr. Mill right; but the mere fact of their antagonism is sufficient to show that the meaning of "the phrase" need not be what Mr. Mill supposes it must be. In fact, "the Absolute" in philosophy always has meant the One as distinguished from the Many, not the One as including the Many. But, as applied to Sir W. Hamilton, Mr. Mill's remarks on "the Absolute," and his subsequent remarks on "the Infinite," not only misrepresent Hamilton's position, but exactly reverse it. Hamilton maintains that the terms "absolute" and "infinite" are perfectly intelligible as abstractions, as much so as "relative" and "finite;" for "correlatives suggest each other," and the "knowledge of contradictories is one;" but he denies that a concrete thing or object can be positively conceived as absolute or infinite. Mr.

Mill represents him as only proving that the "unmeaning abstractions are unknowable,"— abstractions which Hamilton does not assert to be unmeaning, and which he regards as knowable in the only sense in which such abstractions can be known, viz., by understanding the meaning of their names.*

"Something infinite," says Mr. Mill, "is a conception which, like most of our complex ideas, contains a negative element, but which contains positive elements also. Infinite space, for instance; is there nothing positive in that? The negative part of this conception is the absence

* This confusion between conceiving a concrete thing and knowing the meaning of abstract terms is as old as Toland's *Christianity not Mysterious*, and, indeed, has its germ, though not its development, in the teaching of his assumed master, Locke. Locke taught that all our knowledge is founded on simple ideas, and that a complex idea is merely an accumulation of simple ones. Hence Toland maintained that no object could be mysterious or inconceivable if the terms in which its several attributes are expressed have ideas corresponding to them. But, in point of fact, no simple idea can be conceived as an object by itself, though the word by which it is signified has a perfectly intelligible meaning.

of bounds. The positive are, the idea of space, and of space greater than any finite space."—(P. 45.)

This definition of *infinite space* is exactly that which Descartes gives us of *indefinite extension*,—" Ita quia non possumus imaginari extensionem tam magnam, quin intelligamus adhuc majorem esse posse, dicemus magnitudinem rerum possibilium esse indefinitam." * So too, Cudworth, — " There appeareth no sufficient ground for this positive infinity of space ; we being certain of no

---

I cannot, *e. g.*, conceive whiteness by itself, though I can conceive a white wall, *i. e.*, whiteness in combination with other attributes in a concrete object. To conceive attributes as coexisting, however, we must conceive them as coexisting in a certain manner ; for an object of conception is not a mere heap of ideas, but an organized whole, whose constituent ideas exist in a particular combination with and relation to each other. To conceive, therefore, we must not only be able to apprehend each idea separately in the abstract, but also the manner in which they may possibly exist in combination with each other.

* *Principia*, i., 26.

more than this, that be the world or any figurative body never so great, it is not impossible but that it might be still greater and greater without end. Which *indefinite increasableness* of body and space seems to be mistaken for a *positive infinity* thereof."* And Locke, a philosopher for whom Mr. Mill will probably have more respect than for Descartes or Cudworth, writes more plainly : "To have actually in the mind the idea of a space infinite, is to suppose the mind already passed over, and actually to have a view of all those repeated ideas of space, which an endless repetition can never totally represent to it,—which carries in it a plain contradiction."† Mr. Mill thus unwittingly illustrates, in his own person, the

* *Intellectual System*, ed. Harrison, vol. iii., p. 131.
† *Essay*, ii., 17, 7.

truth of Hamilton's remark, " If we dream of effecting this [conceiving the infinite in time or space], we only deceive ourselves by substituting the *indefinite* for the infinite, than which no two notions can be more opposed." In fact, Mr. Mill does not seem to be aware that what the mathematician calls *infinite*, the metaphysician calls *indefinite*, and that arguments drawn from the mathematical use of the term *infinite* are wholly irrelevant to the metaphysical. How, indeed, could it be otherwise? Can any man suppose that, when the Divine attributes are spoken of as infinite, it is meant that they are indefinitely increasable ?*

* One of the ablest mathematicians, and the most persevering Hamiltono-mastix of the day, maintains the applicability of the metaphysical notion of infinity to mathematical magnitudes; but with an assumption which unintentionally vindicates Hamilton's position more fully than could have been done by a professed dis-

In fact, it is the "concrete reality," the "something infinite," and not the mere abstraction of infinity, which is only conceivable as a negation. Every "something" that has ever been intuitively present to my consciousness is a something finite. When, therefore, I speak of a "something infinite,"

---

ciple. "I shall assume," says Professor De Morgan, in a paper recently printed among the *Transactions of the Cambridge Philosophical Society*, "the notion of infinity and of its reciprocal infinitesimal: that a line can be conceived infinite, and therefore having points at an infinite distance. Image apart, which we cannot have, it seems to me clear that a line of infinite length, without points at an infinite distance, is a contradiction." Now it is easy to show, by mere reasoning, without any image, that this assumption is equally a contradiction. For if space is finite, every line in space must be finite also ; and if space is infinite, every point in space must have infinite space beyond it in every direction, and therefore cannot be at the greatest possible distance from another point. Or thus : Any two points in space are the extremities of the line connecting them ; but an infinite line has no extremities ; therefore no two points in space can be connected together by an infinite line.

I mean a something existing in a different manner from all the "somethings" of which I have had experience in intuition. Thus it is apprehended, not positively, but negatively —not directly by what it is, but indirectly by what it is not. A negative idea is not negative because it is expressed by a negative term, but because it has never been realised in intuition. If infinity, as applied to space, means the same thing as being greater than any finite space, both conceptions are equally positive or equally negative. If it does not mean the same thing, then, in conceiving a space greater than any finite space, we do not conceive an infinite space.

7 Mr. Mill's next string of criticisms may be very briefly dismissed. First, Hamilton does *not*, as Mr. Mill asserts, say that "the Unconditioned is inconceivable, because it

includes both the Infinite and the Absolute, and these are contradictory of one another." His argument is a common disjunctive syllogism. The unconditioned, if conceivable at all, must be conceived *either* as the absolute or as the infinite; neither of these is possible; therefore the unconditioned is not conceivable at all. Nor, secondly, is Sir W. Hamilton guilty of the "strange confusion of ideas" which Mr. Mill ascribes to him, when he says that the Absolute, as being absolutely One, cannot be known under the conditions of plurality and difference. The absolute, as such, must be out of all relation, and consequently cannot be conceived in the relation of plurality. "The plurality required," says Mr. Mill, "is not within the thing itself, but is made up between itself and other things." It is, in fact, both;

but even granting Mr. Mill's assumption, what is a "plurality between a thing and other things" but a relation between them? There is undoubtedly a "strange confusion of ideas" in this paragraph; but the confusion is not on the part of Sir W. Hamilton. "Again," continues Mr. Mill, "even if we concede that a thing cannot be known at all unless known as plural, does it follow that it cannot be known as plural because it is also One? Since when have the One and the Many been incompatible things, instead of different aspects of the same thing? . . . If there is any meaning in the words, must not Absolute Unity be Absolute Plurality likewise?" Mr. Mill's "since when?" may be answered in the words of Plato:—"Οὐδὲν ἔμοιγε ἄτοπον δοκεῖ εἶναι εἰ ἓν ἅπαντα ἀποφαίνει τις τῷ μετέχειν τοῦ ἑνὸς καὶ ταὐτὰ ταῦτα πολλὰ τῷ πλήθους αὖ μετέχειν· ἀλλ' εἰ ὃ ἔστιν ἕν, αὐτὸ τοῦτο πολλὰ ἀποδείξει, καὶ αὖ τὰ πολλὰ δὴ ἕν, τοῦτο ἤδη θαυμάσομαι."* Here we are expressly told that "absolute unity" cannot be "absolute plurality." Mr. Mill may say that Plato is wrong; but he will hardly go so far as to say that there is no meaning in his words. In point of fact, however, it is Mr. Mill who is in error, and not Plato. In different relations, no doubt, the same concrete object may be regarded as one or as many. The same measure is one foot or twelve inches; the same sum is one shilling or twelve pence; but it no more follows that "absolute unity must be absolute plurality likewise," than it follows from the above instances that one is equal to twelve. And, thirdly, when Mr. Mill accuses Sir W.

* *Parmenides*, p. 129.

Hamilton of departing from his own meaning of the term *absolute*, in maintaining that the Absolute cannot be a Cause, he only shows that he does not himself know what Hamilton's meaning is. " If Absolute," he says, "means finished, perfected, completed, may there not be a finished, perfected, and completed Cause ?" Hamilton's Absolute is that which is "*out of relation*, as finished, perfect, complete;" and a Cause, as such, is both in relation and incomplete. It is in relation to its effect ; and it is incomplete without its effect. Finally, when Mr. Mill charges Sir W. Hamilton with maintaining " that extension and figure are of the essence of matter, and perceived as such by intuition," we must briefly reply that Hamilton does no such thing. He is not speaking of the essence of matter *per se*, but only of matter as apprehended in relation to us.

Mr. Mill concludes this chapter with an attempt to discover the meaning of Hamilton's assertion, "to think is to condition." We have already explained what Hamilton meant by this expression; and we recur to the subject now, only to show the easy manner in which Mr. Mill manages to miss the point of an argument with the clue lying straight before him. "Did any," he says (of those who say that the Absolute is thinkable), "profess to think it in any other manner than by distinguishing it from other things?" Now this is the very thing which, according to Hamilton, Schelling actually did. Mr. Mill does not attempt to show that Hamilton is wrong in his interpretation of Schelling, nor, if he is right, what were the reasons which led Schelling to so paradoxical a position : he simply assumes that no man could hold Schelling's view, and there is an end of it.* Hamilton's purpose is to reassert in substance the doctrine which Kant maintained, and which Schelling denied ; and the natural way to ascertain his meaning would be by reference to these two philosophers. But this is not the method of

---

* Mr. Mill does not expressly name Schelling in this sentence; but he does so shortly afterwards; and his remark is of the same character with the previous one. "Even Schelling," he says, "was not so gratuitously absurd as to deny that the Absolute must be known according to the capacities of that which knows it—though he was forced to invent a special capacity for the purpose." But if this capacity is an "invention" of Schelling's, and if he was "forced" to invent it, Hamilton's point is proved. To think, according to all the real operations of thought which consciousness makes known to us, is to condition. And the faculty of the unconditioned is an invention of Schelling's, not known to consciousness. In other words : all our real faculties bear witness to the truth of Hamilton's statement; and the only way of controverting it is to invent an imaginary faculty for the purpose.

Mr. Mill, here or elsewhere. He generally endeavours to ascertain Hamilton's meaning by ranging the wide field of possibilities. He tells us what a phrase means in certain authors of whom Hamilton is not thinking, or in reference to certain matters which Hamilton is not discussing; but he hardly ever attempts to trace the history of Hamilton's own view, or the train of thought by which it suggested itself to his mind. And the result of this is, that Mr. Mill's interpretations are generally in the potential mood. He wastes a good deal of conjecture in discovering what Hamilton might have meant, when a little attention in the right quarter would have shown what he did mean.

The third feature of Hamilton's philosophy which we charged Mr. Mill with misunderstanding, is the distinction between Knowledge and Belief. In the early part of this article, we endeavoured to explain the true nature of this distinction; we have now only a very limited space to notice Mr. Mill's criticisms on it. Hamilton, he says, admitted "a second source of intellectual conviction called Belief." Now Belief is not a "source" of any conviction, but the conviction itself. No man would say that he is convinced of the truth of a proposition *because* he believes it; his belief in its truth is the same thing as his conviction of its truth. Belief, then, is not a source of conviction, but a conviction having sources of its own. The question is, have we legitimate sources of conviction, distinct from those which constitute Knowledge properly so called? Now here it should be remembered that the distinction is not one invented by Hamilton to meet the exigencies of his own system. He enumerates as many as twenty-two authors, of the most various schools of philosophy, who all acknowledged it before him. Such a concurrence is no slight argument in favour of the reality of the distinction. We do not say that these writers, or Hamilton himself, have always expressed this distinction in the best language, or applied it in the best manner; but we say that it is a true distinction, and that it is valid for the principal purpose to which Hamilton applied it.

We do not agree with all the details of Hamilton's application. We do not agree with him, though he is supported by very eminent authorities, in classifying our conviction of axiomatic principles as *belief*, and not as *knowledge*.* But this question does not directly bear on Mr. Mill's criticism. The point of that criticism is, that Hamilton, by admitting a *belief* in the infinite and unrelated, nullifies his own doctrine, that all *knowledge* is of the finite and relative. Let us see.

* Hamilton's distinction is in principle the same as that which we have given in our previous remarks (pp. 18, 19). He says, "A conviction is incomprehensible when there is merely given to us in consciousness—*That its object is* (ὅτι ἔστι), and when we are unable to comprehend through a higher notion or belief *Why or How it is* (διότι ἔστι)."—(*Reid's Works*, p. 754.) We would distinguish between *why* and *how*, between διότι and πῶς. We can give no reason *why* two straight lines cannot enclose a space; but we can comprehend *how* they cannot. We have only to form the corresponding image, to see the manner in which the two attributes coexist in one object. But when I say that I believe in the existence of a spiritual being who sees without eyes, I cannot conceive the *manner* in which seeing coexists with the absence of the bodily organ of sight. We believe that the true distinction between knowledge and belief may ultimately be referred to the presence or absence of the corresponding intuition; but to show this in the various instances would require a longer dissertation than our present limits will allow.

We may believe *that* a thing is, without being able to conceive *how* it is. I believe *that* God is a person, and also *that* He is infinite; though I cannot conceive *how* the attributes of personality and infinity exist together. All my knowledge of personality is derived from my consciousness of my own finite personality. I therefore believe in the coexistence of attributes in God, in some manner different from that in which they coexist in me as limiting each other: and thus I believe in the fact, though I am unable to conceive the manner. So, again, Kant brings certain counter arguments, to prove, on the one side, that the world has a beginning in time, and, on the other side, that it has not a beginning. Now suppose I am unable to refute either of these courses of argument, am I therefore compelled to have no belief at all? May I not say, I believe, in spite of Kant, *that* the world has a beginning in time, though I am unable to conceive *how* it can have so begun? What is this, again, but a belief in an absolute reality beyond the sphere of my relative knowledge?

"I am not now considering," says Mr Mill, "what it is that, in our author's opinion, we are bound to believe concerning the unknowable." Why, this was the very thing he ought to have considered, before pronouncing the position to be untenable, or to be irreconcilable with something else Meanwhile, it is instructive to observe that Mr. Mill himself believes, or requires his readers to believe, something concerning the unknown. He does not know, or at any rate he does not tell his readers, what Hamilton requires them to believe concerning the unknowable; but he himself believes, and requires them to believe, that this unknown something is incompatible with the doctrine that knowledge is relative. We cannot regard this as a very satisfactory mode of refuting Hamilton's thesis.*

---

* In a subsequent chapter (p. 120), Mr. Mill endeavours to overthrow this distinction between Knowledge and Belief, by means of Hamilton's own theory of Consciousness. Hamilton maintains that we cannot be conscious of a mental operation without being conscious of its object. On this Mr. Mill retorts that if, as Hamilton admits, we are conscious of a belief in the Infinite and the Absolute, we must be conscious of the Infinite and the Absolute themselves; and such consciousness is Knowledge. The fallacy of this retort is transparent. The immediate object of Belief is a *proposition* which I hold to be true, not a *thing* apprehended in an act of conception. I believe in an infinite God; *i.e.*, I believe *that* God is infinite: I believe that the attributes which I ascribe to God exist in Him in an infinite degree. Now, to believe this proposition, I must, of course, be conscious of its meaning; but I am not therefore conscious of the Infinite God as an object of conception; for this would require further an apprehension of the manner in which these infinite attributes coexist so as to form one object. The whole argument of this eighth chapter is confused, owing to

I

But if Mr. Mill is unjust towards the distinction between Knowledge and Belief, as held by Sir W. Hamilton, he makes ample amends to the injured theory in the next chapter, by enlarging the province of credibility far beyond any extent which Hamilton would have dreamed of claiming for it. Conceivability or inconceivablity, he tells us, are usually dependent on association; and it is quite possible that, under other associations, we might be able to conceive, and therefore to believe, anything short of the direct contradiction that the same thing is and is not. It is not in itself incredible that a square may at the same time be

---

Mr. Mill not having distinguished between those passages in which Sir W. Hamilton is merely using an *argumentum ad hominem* in relation to Reid, and those in which he is reasoning from general principles.

The Philosophy of the Conditioned. 131

round, that two straight lines may enclose a space, or even that two and two may make five.* But whatever concessions Mr. Mill may make on this point, he is at least fully determined that Sir W. Hamilton shall derive no benefit from them; for he forthwith proceeds to charge Sir William with confusing three distinct senses of the term *conception*—a confusion which exists solely in his own imagination,†—and to assert that

---

* In reference to this last paradox, Mr. Mill quotes from *Essays by a Barrister:* "There is a world in which, whenever two pairs of things are either placed in proximity or are contemplated together, a fifth thing is immediately created and brought within the contemplation of the mind engaged in putting two and two together. . . . In such a world surely two and two would make five. That is, the result to the mind of contemplating two twos would be to count five." The answer to this reasoning has been already given by Archdeacon Lee in his Essay on Miracles. The "five" in this case is not the sum of two and two, but of two and two *plus* the new creature, *i.e.*, of two and two *plus* one.

† The sense in which Sir W. Hamilton himself uses the word *conception* is explained in a note to *Reid's Works*, p. 377—namely,

the Philosophy of the Conditioned is entirely founded on a mistake, inasmuch as infinite space on the one hand, and, on the other, both an absolute minimum and an infinite divisibility of space, are perfectly conceivable. With regard to the former of these two assertions, Mr. Mill's whole argument is

---

the combination of two or more attributes in a *unity of representation*. The second sense which Mr. Mill imagines is simply a mistake of his own. When Hamilton speaks of being "unable to conceive as possible," he does not mean, as Mr. Mill supposes, physically possible under the law of gravitation or some other law of matter, but mentally possible as a representation or image ; and thus the supposed second sense is identical with the first. The third sense may also be reduced to the first ; for to conceive two attributes as combined in one representation is to form a notion subordinate to those of each attribute separately. We do not say that Sir W. Hamilton has been uniformly accurate in his application of the test of conceivability ; but we say that his inaccuracies, such as they are, do not affect the theory of the conditioned, and that in all the long extracts which Mr. Mill quotes, with footnotes, indicating "first sense," "second sense," "third sense," the author's meaning may be more accurately explained in the first sense only.

vitiated, as we have already shown, by his confusion between *infinite* and *indefinite*; but it is worth while to quote one of his special instances in this chapter, as a specimen of the kind of reasoning which an eminent writer on logic can sometimes employ. In reference to Sir W. Hamilton's assertion, that infinite space would require infinite time to conceive it, he says, " Let us try the doctrine upon a complex whole, short of infinite, such as the number 695,788. Sir W. Hamilton would not, I suppose, have maintained that this number is inconceivable. How long did he think it would take to go over every separate unit of this whole, so as to obtain a perfect knowledge of the exact sum, as different from all other sums, either greater or less?"

It is marvellous that it should not have

occurred to Mr. Mill, while he was writing this passage, "How comes this large number to be a 'whole' at all; and how comes it that 'this whole,' with all its units, can be written down by means of six digits?" Simply because of a conventional arrangement, by which a single digit, according to its position, can express, by one mark, tens, hundreds, thousands, &c., of units; and thus can exhaust the sum by dealing with its items in large masses. But how can such a process exhaust the infinite? We should like to know how long Mr. Mill thinks it would take to work out the following problem:—
"If two figures can represent ten, three a hundred, four a thousand, five ten thousand, &c., find the number of figures required to represent infinity."*

---

* Precisely the same misconception of Hamilton's position occurs

Infinite divisibility stands or falls with infinite extension. In both cases Mr. Mill confounds infinity with indefiniteness. But with regard to an absolute minimum of space, Mr. Mill's argument requires a separate notice.

"It is not denied," he says, "that there is a portion of extension which to the naked eye appears an indivisible point; it has been called by philosophers the *minimum visibile*. This minimum we can indefinitely magnify by means of optical instruments, making visible the still smaller parts which compose it. In each successive experiment there is still a *minimum visibile*, anything less than which cannot be discovered with that instrument, but can with one of a higher power. Suppose, now, that

---

in Professor De Morgan's paper in the *Cambridge Transactions*, to which we have previously referred. He speaks (p. 13) of the "notion, which runs through many writers, from Descartes to Hamilton, that the mind must be big enough to *hold* all it can conceive." This notion is certainly not maintained by Hamilton, nor yet by Descartes in the paragraph quoted by Mr. De Morgan; nor, as far as we are aware, in any other part of his works.

as we increase the magnifying power of our instruments, and before we have reached the limit of possible increase, we arrive at a stage at which that which seemed the smallest visible space under a given microscope, does not appear larger under one which, by its mechanical construction, is adapted to magnify more, but still remains apparently indivisible. I say, that if this happened, we should believe in a minimum of extension; or if some *à priori* metaphysical prejudice prevented us from believing it, we should at least be enabled to conceive it."—(P. 84.)

The natural conclusion of most men under such circumstances would be, that there was some fault in the microscope. But even if this conclusion were rejected, we presume Mr. Mill would allow that, under the supposed circumstances, the exact magnitude of the minimum of extension would be calculable. We have only to measure the *minimum visibile*, and know what is the magnifying power of our microscope, to determine the exact dimensions. Suppose, then, that we assign to it some definite magnitude—say the ten billionth part of an inch,—should we then conclude that it is impossible to conceive the twenty billionth part of an inch?—in other words, that we have arrived at a definite magnitude which has no conceivable half? Surely this is a somewhat rash concession to be made by a writer who has just told us that numbers may be conceived up to infinity; and therefore, of course, down to infinitesimality.

Mr. Mill concludes this chapter with an assertion which, even by itself, is sufficient to show how very little he has attended to or understood the philosophy which he is attempting to criticise. "The law of Excluded Middle," he says, "as well as that of Contradiction, is common to all phenomena.

But it is a doctrine of our author that these laws are true, and cannot but be known to be true, of Noumena likewise. It is not merely Space as cognisable by our senses, but Space as it is in itself, which he affirms must be either of unlimited or of limited extent" (p. 86). At this sentence we fairly stand aghast. "Space as it is in itself!" the Noumenon Space! Has Mr. Mill been all this while "examining" Sir William Hamilton's philosophy, in utter ignorance that the object of that philosophy is the "Conditioned in Time and *Space;*" that he accepts Kant's analysis of time and space as formal necessities of thought, but pronounces no opinion whatever as to whether time and space can exist as Noumena or not? It is the phenomenal space, "space as cognisable by our senses," which Sir W. Hamilton says must be either limited or unlimited: concerning the Noumenon Space, he does not hazard an opinion whether such a thing exists or not. He says, indeed (and this is probably what has misled Mr. Mill), that the laws of Identity, Contradiction, and Excluded Middle, are laws of things as well as laws of thought;* but he says nothing about these laws as predicating infinite or finite extension. On the contrary, he expressly classifies Space under the law of Relativity, the violation of which indicates what may exist, but what we are unable to conceive as existing. Briefly, the law of Excluded Middle (to take this instance alone) is a law of things only in its abstract form, "Everything must be A or not A" (*extended*, if you please, or *not extended*); but in its subordi-

* *Discussions*, p. 603.

nate form, "Everything extended must be extended infinitely or finitely," it is only applicable, and only intended by Hamilton to be applied, to those *phenomena* which are already given as extended in some degree.

We have now examined the first six chapters of Mr. Mill's book, containing his remarks on that portion of Sir W. Hamilton's philosophy which he justly regards as comprising the most important of the doctrines which specially belong to Hamilton himself. The next chapter is an episode, in which Mr. Mill turns aside from Sir W. Hamilton to criticise Mr. Mansel's *Bampton Lectures*. As our limits do not permit us to carry on the argument at present through the remainder of Mr. Mill's remarks on Hamilton himself, we shall conclude our notice with a few words on this chapter, as closing the properly metaphysical portion of Mr. Mill's book, and as affording ample proof that, in this department of philosophy at least, Mr. Mill's powers of misapprehension do not cease when Sir W. Hamilton is no longer their object.

Mr. Mill's method of criticism makes it generally necessary to commence with a statement of the criticised theory as it really is, before proceeding to his exposition of it as it is not. The present instance offers no exception to this rule. Mr. Mansel's argument may be briefly stated as follows. The primary and essential conception of God, imperatively demanded by our moral and religious consciousness, is that of a *person*. But personality implies intellectual and moral attributes; and the only direct and immediate knowledge which we have of such attributes is derived from the testimony of self-consciousness, bearing witness to their existence in a certain manner in ourselves. But when we endeavour to transfer the conception of personality, thus obtained, to the domain of theology, we meet with certain difficulties, which, while they are not sufficient to hinder us from *believing* in the Divine Personality as a fact, yet hinder us from *conceiving* the manner of its existence, and prevent us from exhibiting our belief as a philosophical conclusion, proved by irrefragable reasoning and secured against all objections. These difficulties are occasioned, on the one hand, by the so-called Philosophy of the Unconditioned, which in all ages has shown a tendency towards Pantheism, and which, in one of its latest and most finished manifestations, announces itself as the exhibition of God as He is in His eternal nature before creation; and, on the other hand, by the limitations and conditions to which our own personality is subject, and which, as we have pointed out in the earlier part of this article, have, from the very beginning of Christian theology, prevented theologians from accepting the limited personality of man as an exact image and counterpart of the unlimited personality of God. These difficulties Mr. Mansel endeavours to meet in two ways. On the one side, he maintains, in common with Sir W. Hamilton, that the Philosophy of the Unconditioned, by reason of its own incongruities and self-contradictions, has no claim to be accepted as a competent witness in the matter; and on the other side, he maintains, in common with many theologians before him, that human personality cannot be assumed as an exact copy of the Divine, but only as that which is most nearly analogous to it among finite things. But these two positions, if admitted, involve a corresponding practical conclusion as regards the criterion of religious truth or falsehood. Were we capable, either, on the one hand, of a clear conception of the Unconditioned, or, on the other, of a direct intuition of the Divine Attributes as objects of consciousness, we might be able to construct, deductively or inductively, an exact science of Theology. As it is, we are compelled to reason by analogy; and analogy furnishes only probabilities, varying, it may be, from slight presumptions up to moral certainties, but whose weight, in any given case, can only be determined by comparison with other evidences. There are three distinct sources from which we may form a judgment about the ways of God—first, from our own moral and intellectual consciousness, by which we judge *à priori* of what God ought to do in a given case, by determining what we should think it wise or right for ourselves to do in a similar case; secondly, from the constitution and course of nature, from which we may learn by experience what God's providence in certain cases actually is; and thirdly, from revelation, attested by its proper evidences. Where these three agree in their testimony (as in the great majority of cases they do) we have the moral certainty which results from the harmony of all accessible evidences: where they appear to differ, we have no right at once to conclude that the second or the third must give way to the first, and not *vice versâ*; because we have no right to assume that the first alone is infallible. In the author's own words: "The lesson to be learnt from an examination of the Limits of Religious Thought is not that man's judgments are *worthless* in relation to Divine things, but that they are *fallible:* and the probability of error in any particular case can never be fairly estimated without giving their full weight to all collateral considerations. We are indeed bound to believe that a Revelation given by God can never contain anything that is really unwise or unrighteous; but we are not always capable of estimating exactly the wisdom or righteousness of particular doctrines or precepts. And we are bound to bear in mind that *exactly in proportion to the strength of the remaining evidence for the Divine origin of a religion, is* the probability that we may be mistaken in supposing this or that portion of its contents to be unworthy of God. Taken in conjunction, the two arguments may confirm or correct each other: taken singly and absolutely, each may vitiate the result which should follow from their joint application." *

In criticising the first part of this argument —that which is directed against the deductive philosophy of the Unconditioned—Mr. Mill manifests the same want of acquaintance with its meaning, and with the previous history of the question, which he had before exhibited in his attack on Sir W. Hamilton. He begins by finding fault with the definition of the Absolute, which Mr. Mansel (herein departing, and purposely departing, from Sir W. Hamilton's use of the term) defines as

* *Bampton Lectures*, p. 156, 4th edition.

"that which exists in and by itself, having no necessary relation to any other Being." On this, Mr. Mill remarks: "The first words of his definition would serve for the description of a Noumenon; but Mr. Mansel's Absolute is only meant to denote one Being, identified with God, and God is not the only Noumenon." The description of a Noumenon! This is almost equal to the discovery of a Noumenon Space. Does Mr. Mill really suppose that all noumena are self-existent? A *noumenon* (in the sense in which we suppose Mr. Mill to understand the term, for it has different meanings in different philosophies) implies an existence out of relation to the human mind.* But is

* Strictly speaking, the term *noumenon*, as meaning that which can be apprehended only by the intellect, implies a relation to the intellect apprehending it; and in this sense τὸ νοούμενον is opposed by Plato to τὸ ὁρώμενον—the object of intellect to the object of

this the same as being out of all relation whatever, as existing "in and by itself?" Does Mr. Mill mean to say that a creature, whether perceived by us or not, has no relation to its Creator? But Mr. Mill, as we have seen before, is not much at home when he gets among "noumena." We must proceed to his criticism of the second part of the definition,—"having no necessary relation to

---

sight. But as the intellect was supposed to take cognisance of things as they are, in opposition to the sensitive perception of things as they appear, the term *noumenon* became synonymous with *thing in itself* (τὸ ὂν καθ' αὑτό). And this meaning is retained in the Kantian philosophy, in which the *noumenon* is identical with the *Ding an sich*. But as Kant denied to the human intellect any immediate intuition of things as they are (though such an intuition may be possible to a superhuman intellect), hence the term *noumenon* in the Kantian philosophy is opposed to all of which the human intellect can take positive cognisance. Hamilton, in this respect, agrees with Kant. But neither Kant nor Hamilton, in opposing the *thing in itself* to the *phenomenon*, meant to imply that the former is necessarily self-existent, and therefore uncreated.

any other being." Of these words he says, that "they admit of two constructions. The words in their natural sense only mean, *capable of existing out of relation to anything else.* The argument requires that they should mean *incapable of existing in relation with anything else.*" And why is this non-natural sense to be forced upon very plain words? Because, says Mr. Mill,—

"In what manner is a possible existence out of all relation, incompatible with the notion of a cause? Have not causes a possible existence apart from their effects? Would the sun, for example, not exist if there were no earth or planets for it to illuminate? Mr. Mansel seems to think that what is capable of existing out of relation, cannot possibly be conceived or known in relation. But this is not so. . . . Freed from this confusion of ideas, Mr. Mansel's argument resolves itself into this,—The same Being cannot be thought by us both as Cause and as Absolute, because a Cause *as such* is not Absolute, and Absolute, as such, is not a Cause; which is exactly as if he had said that Newton cannot be thought by us both as an Englishman and as a mathematician, because an Englishman, as such, is not a mathematician, nor a mathematician, as such, an Englishman."—(P. 92.)

The "confusion of ideas" is entirely of Mr. Mill's own making, and is owing to his having mutilated the argument before criticising it. The argument in its original form consists of two parts; the first intended to show that the Absolute is not conceived *as such* in being conceived as a Cause; the second to show that the Absolute cannot be conceived under different aspects at different times—first as Absolute, and then as Cause. It was the impossibility of this latter alternative which drove Cousin to the hypothesis of a necessary causation from all eternity. Mr. Mill entirely omits the latter part of the argument, and treats the former part as if it were the whole. The part criticised by Mr. Mill is intended to prove exactly what it does prove, and no more; namely, that a cause *as such* is not the absolute, and that to know a cause *as such* is not to know the absolute. We presume Mr. Mill himself will admit that to know Newton as a mathematician is not to know him as an Englishman. Whether he can be known separately as both, and whether the Absolute in this respect is a parallel case, depends on another consideration, which Mr. Mill has not noticed. The continuation of Mr. Mill's criticism is equally confused. He says :—

"The whole of Mr. Mansel's argument for the inconceivability of the Infinite and of the Absolute is one long *ignoratio elenchi*. It has been pointed out in a former chapter that the words Absolute and Infinite have no real meaning, unless we understand by them that which is

The Philosophy of the Conditioned. 153

absolute or infinite in some given attribute; as space is called infinite, meaning that it is infinite in extension; and as God is termed infinite, in the sense of possessing infinite power, and absolute in the sense of absolute goodness or knowledge. It has also been shown that Sir W. Hamilton's arguments for the unknowableness of the Unconditioned do not prove that we cannot know an object which is absolute or infinite in some specific attribute, but only that we cannot know an abstraction called 'The Absolute' or 'The Infinite,' which is supposed to have all attributes at once."—(P. 93.)

The fallacy of this criticism, as regards Sir W. Hamilton, has been already pointed out: as regards Mr. Mansel, it is still more glaring, inasmuch as that writer expressly states that he uses the term *absolute* in a different sense from that which Mr. Mill attributes to Sir W. Hamilton. When Mr. Mill charges Mr. Mansel with "undertaking to prove the impossibility" of conceiving "a

Being *absolutely* just or *absolutely* wise"* (*i. e.*, as he supposes, *perfectly* just or wise), he actually forgets that he has just been criticising Mr. Mansel's definition of the Absolute, as something having a possible existence "out of all relation." Will Mr. Mill have the kindness to tell us what he means by goodness and knowledge "out of all relation;" *i.e.*, a goodness and knowledge related to no object on which they can be exercised; a goodness which is good to nothing, a knowledge which knows nothing? Mr. Mill had better be cautious in talking about *ignoratio elenchi*.

From the Absolute, Mr. Mill proceeds to the Infinite; and here he commits the same mistake as before, treating a portion of an argument as if it were the whole, and citing

* *Examination*, p. 95.

a portion intended to prove one point as if it were intended to prove another. He cites a passage from Mr. Mansel, in which it is said that "the Infinite, if it is to be conceived at all, must be conceived as potentially everything and actually nothing; for if there is anything in general which it cannot become, it is thereby limited; and if there is anything in particular which it actually is, it is thereby excluded from being any other thing. But, again, it must also be conceived as actually everything and potentially nothing; for an unrealised potentiality is likewise a limitation. If the Infinite can be that which it is not, it is by that very possibility marked out as incomplete, and capable of a higher perfection. If it is actually everything, it possesses no characteristic feature by which it can be distinguished from anything else, and discerned as an object of consciousness." On this passage Mr. Mill remarks, "Can a writer be serious who bids us conjure up a conception of something which possesses infinitely all conflicting attributes, and because we cannot do this without contradiction, would have us believe that there is a contradiction in the idea of infinite goodness or infinite wisdom?" The answer to this criticism is very simple. The argument is not employed for the purpose which Mr. Mill supposes. It is employed to show that the metaphysical notion of the absolute-infinite, as the sum, potential or actual, of all possible existence, is inconceivable under the laws of human consciousness; and thus that the absolutely first existence, related to nothing and limited by nothing, the *ens realissimum* of the older philosophers, the *pure being* of the Hegelians, cannot be attained as a starting-point from which to deduce all relative and derived existence. How far the empirical conception of certain mental attributes, such as goodness or wisdom, derived in the first instance from our own personal consciousness, can be positively conceived as extended to infinity, is considered in a separate argument, which Mr. Mill does not notice.

Mr. Mill continues, " Instead of 'the Infinite,' substitute 'an infinitely good Being' [*i. e.*, substitute what is not intended], and Mr. Mansel's argument reads thus : — ' If there is anything which an infinitely good Being cannot become—if he cannot become bad—that is a limitation, and the goodness cannot be infinite. If there is anything which an infinitely good Being actually is (namely, good), he is excluded from being any other thing, as being wise or powerful.'" To the first part of this objection we reply by simply asking, "Is becoming bad a 'higher perfection?'" To the second part we reply by Mr. Mill's favourite mode of reasoning—a parallel case. A writer asserts that a creature which is a horse is thereby excluded from being a dog; and that, in so far as it has the nature of a horse, it has not the nature of a dog. "What!" exclaims Mr. Mill, "is it not the nature of a dog to have four legs? and does the man mean to say that a horse has not four legs?" We venture respectfully to ask Mr. Mill whether he supposes that being wise is being "a thing," and being good is being another "thing?"

But, seriously, it is much to be wished that when a writer like Mr. Mill undertakes to discuss philosophical questions, he should acquire some slight acquaintance with the history of the questions discussed. Had this been done by our critic in the present case, it might possibly have occurred to him to doubt whether a doctrine supported by philosophers of such different schools of thought as Spinoza, Malebranche, Wolf, Kant, Schelling, could be quite such a piece of transparent nonsense as he supposes it to be. All these writers are cited in Mr. Mansel's note, as maintaining the theory that the Absolute is the *ens realissimum*, or sum of all existence; and their names might have saved Mr. Mill from the absurdity of supposing that by this expression was meant something "absolutely good and absolutely bad; absolutely wise and absolutely stupid; and so forth." The real meaning of the expression has been already sufficiently explained in our earlier remarks. The problem of the Philosophy of the Unconditioned, as sketched by Plato and generally adopted by subsequent philosophers, is, as we have seen, to ascend up to the first principle of all things, and thence to deduce, as from their cause, all dependent and derived existences. The Unconditioned, as the one first principle, must necessarily contain in itself, potentially or actually, all that is derived from it, and thus must comprehend, in embryo or in development, the sum of all existence. To reconcile this conclusion with the phenomenal existence of evil and imperfection, is the difficulty with which philosophy has had to struggle ever since philosophy began. The Manichean, by referring evil to an independent cause, denies the existence of an absolute first principle at all; the Leibnitzian, with his hypothesis of the best possible world, virtually sets bounds to the Divine omnipotence: the Pantheist identifies God with all actual existence, and either denies the real existence of evil at all, or merges the distinction between evil and good in some higher indifference. All these conclusions may be alike untenable, but all alike testify to the existence of the problem, and to the vast though unsuccessful efforts which man's reason has made to solve it.

The reader may now, perhaps, understand the reason of an assertion which Mr. Mill regards as supremely absurd,—namely, that we must believe in the existence of an absolute and infinite Being, though unable to conceive the nature of such a Being. To believe in such a Being, is simply to believe that God made the world: to declare the nature of such a Being inconceivable, is simply to say that we do not know how the world was made. If we believe that God made the world, we must believe that there was a time when the world was not, and when God alone existed, out of relation to any other being. But the mode of that sole existence we are unable to conceive, nor in what manner the first act took place by which the absolute and self-existent gave existence to the relative and dependent. "The contradictions," says Mr. Mill, "which Mr. Mansel asserts to be involved in the notions, do not follow from an imperfect mode of apprehending the Infinite and the Absolute, but lie in the definitions of them, in the meaning of the words themselves." They do no such thing: the meaning of the words is perfectly intelligible, and is exactly what is expressed by their definitions : the contradictions arise from the attempt to combine the attributes expressed by the words in one representation with others, so as to form a positive object of consciousness. Where is the incongruity of saying, " I believe that a being exists possessing certain attributes, though I am unable in my present state of knowledge to conceive the manner of that existence ?" Mr. Mill, at all events, is the last man in the world who has any right to complain of such a distinction—Mr. Mill, who considers it not incredible that in some part of the universe two straight lines may enclose a space, or two and two make five ; though he is compelled to allow that under our present laws of thought, or, if he pleases, of association, we are unable to conceive how these things can be.

It is wearisome work to wade through this mass of misconceptions; yet we must entreat the reader's patience a little longer, while we say a few words in conclusion on perhaps the greatest misconception of all—though that is bold language to use with regard to Mr. Mill's metaphysics,—at any rate, the one which he expresses in the most vehement language. Mr. Mansel, as we have said, asserts, as many others have asserted before him, that the relation between the communicable attributes of God and the corresponding attributes of man is one not of identity, but of analogy; that is to say, that the Divine attributes have the same relation to the Divine nature that the human attributes have to human nature. Thus, for example, there is a Divine justice and there is a human justice; but God is just as the

Creator and Governor of the world, having unlimited authority over all His creatures and unlimited jurisdiction over all their acts; and man is just in certain special relations, as having authority over some persons and some acts only, so far as is required for the needs of human society. So, again, there is a Divine mercy and there is a human mercy; but God is merciful in such a manner as is fitting compatibly with the righteous government of the universe; and man is merciful in a certain limited range, the exercise of the attribute being guided by considerations affecting the welfare of society or of individuals. Or to take a more general case: Man has in himself a rule of right and wrong, implying subjection to the authority of a superior (for conscience has authority only as reflecting the law of God); while

God has in Himself a rule of right and wrong, implying no higher authority, and determined absolutely by His own nature. The case is the same when we look at moral attributes, not externally, in their active manifestations, but internally, in their psychological constitution. If we do not attribute to God the same complex mental constitution of reason, passion, and will, the same relation to motives and inducements, the same deliberation and choice of alternatives, the same temporal succession of facts in consciousness, which we ascribe to man,— it will follow that those psychological relations between reason, will, and desire, which are implied in the conception of human action, cannot represent the Divine excellences in themselves, but can only illustrate them by analogies from finite things. And if man is liable to error in judging of the conduct of his fellow-men, in proportion as he is unable to place himself in their position, or to realise to himself their modes of thought and principles of action—if the child, for instance, is liable to error in judging the actions of the man,—or the savage of the civilised man,—surely there is far more room for error in men's judgment of the ways of God, in proportion as the difference between God and man is greater than the difference between a man and a child.

This doctrine elicits from Mr. Mill the following extraordinary outburst of rhetoric :—

" If, instead of the glad tidings that there exists a Being in whom all the excellences which the highest human mind can conceive, exist in a degree inconceivable to us, I am informed that the world is ruled by a being whose attributes are infinite, but what they are we cannot learn, nor what are the principles of his government, except that 'the highest human morality which we are capable of conceiving' does not sanction them; convince me of it, and I will bear my fate as I may. But when I am told that I must believe this, and at the same time call this being by the names which express and affirm the highest human morality, I say in plain terms that I will not. Whatever power such a being may have over me, there is one thing which he shall not do: he shall not compel me to worship him. I will call no being good, who is not what I mean when I apply that epithet to my fellow-creatures; and if such a being can sentence me to hell for not so calling him, to hell I will go."—(P. 103.)

We will not pause to comment on the temper and taste of this declamation; we will simply ask whether Mr. Mill really supposes the word *good* to lose all community of meaning, when it is applied, as it constantly is, to different persons among our "fellow-creatures," with express reference to their different duties and different qualifications for performing them? The duties of a father are not the same as those of a son; is the word therefore wholly equivocal when we speak of one person as a *good father*, and another as a *good son*? Nay, when we speak generally of a man as *good*, has not the epithet a tacit reference to human nature and human duties? and yet is there no community of meaning when the same epithet is applied to other creatures? Ἡ ἀρετὴ πρὸς τὸ ἔργον τὸ οἰκεῖον,—the goodness of any being whatever has relation to the nature and office of that being. We may therefore test Mr. Mill's declamation by a parallel case. A wise and experienced father addresses a young and inexperienced son: "My son," he says, "there may be some of my actions which do not seem to you to be wise or good, or such as you would do in my place. Remember, however, that your duties are different from mine; that your knowledge of my duties is very imperfect; and that there may be things which you cannot now see to be wise and good, but which you may hereafter discover to be so." "Father," says the son, "your principles of action are not the same as mine; the highest morality which I can conceive at present does not sanction them; and as for believing that you are good in anything of which I do not plainly see the goodness,"—We will not repeat Mr. Mill's alternative; we will only ask whether it is not just possible that there may be as much difference between man and God as there is between a child and his father?

This declamation is followed by a sneer, which is worth quoting, not on its own account, but as an evidence of the generosity with which Mr. Mill deals with the supposed motives of his antagonists, and of the accuracy of his acquaintance with the subject discussed. He says :—

"It is worthy of remark, that the doubt whether words applied to God have their human signification, is only felt when the words relate to his moral attributes; it is never heard of with regard to his power. We are never told that God's omnipotence must not be supposed to mean an infinite degree of the power we know in man and nature, and that perhaps it does not mean that he is able to kill us, or consign us to eternal flames. The Divine Power is always interpreted in a completely human signification; but the Divine Goodness and Justice must be understood to be such only in an unintelligible sense. Is it unfair to surmise that this is because those who speak in the name of God, have need of the human conception of his power, since an idea which can overawe and enforce obedience must address itself to real feelings; but are content that his goodness should be conceived only as something inconceivable, because they are so often required to teach doctrines respecting him which conflict irreconcilably with all goodness that we can conceive?"—(P. 104.)

On the latter part of this paragraph we will not attempt to comment. But as regards the former part, we meet Mr. Mill's confident assertion with a direct denial, and take the opportunity of informing him that the conception of infinite Power has suggested the same difficulties, and has been discussed by philosophers and theologians in the same manner, as those of infinite Wisdom and infinite Goodness. Has Mr. Mill never heard of such questions as, Whether Omnipotence can reverse the past?—Whether God can do that which He does not will to do?—Whether God's perfect foreknowledge is compatible with his own perfect liberty?—Whether God could have made a better world than the existing one? Nay, has not

The Philosophy of the Conditioned. 173

our critic, in this very chapter, been arguing against Mr. Mansel on the question, whether the Absolute can be conceived as a Cause acting in time : and what is this but a form of the question, whether power, when predicated of God is exactly the same thing as power when predicated of man ? Or why has it been said that creation *ex nihilo*—an absolutely first act of causation, is inconceivable by us, but from the impossibility of finding in human power an exact type of Divine power ? To attribute discreditable motives to an opponent, even to account for unquestionable facts, is usually considered as an abuse of criticism. What shall we say when the facts are fictitious as well as the motives ? With regard to Mr. Mansel, the only person who is included by name in this accusation, it is " worthy of remark," that the earliest mention of the obnoxious theory in his writings occurs in connection with a difficulty relating solely to the conception of infinite power, and not at all to the moral attributes of God.*

Mr. Mill concludes this chapter with another instance of that *ignoratio elenchi* which has been so abundantly manifested throughout his previous criticisms. His opponent, he allows, "would and does admit that the qualities as conceived by us bear *some likeness* to the justice and goodness which belong to God, since man was made in God's image." But he considers that this "semi-concession" "destroys the whole fabric" of Mr. Mansel's argument. "The Divine goodness," he says, "which is said to be a different thing from human goodness,

---

* See *Prolegomena Logica*, p. 77 (2nd ed., p. 85.)

but of which the human conception of goodness is some imperfect reflexion or resemblance, does it agree with what men call goodness in the *essence* of the quality—in what *constitutes* it goodness? If it does, the 'Rationalists' are right; it is not illicit to reason from the one to the other. If not, the divine attribute, whatever else it may be, is not goodness, and ought not to be called by the name." Now the question really at issue is not whether the " Rationalist" argument is licit or illicit, but whether, in its lawful use, it is to be regarded as infallible or fallible. We have already quoted a portion of Mr. Mansel's language on this point; we will now quote two more passages, which, without any comment, will sufficiently show how utterly Mr. Mill has mistaken the purport of the argument which he has undertaken to examine.

"We do not certainly know the exact nature and operation of the moral attributes of God: we can but infer and conjecture from what we know of the moral attributes of man: and the analogy between the Finite and the Infinite can never be so perfect as to preclude all possibility of error in the process. But the possibility becomes almost a certainty, when any one human faculty is elevated by itself into an authoritative criterion of religious truth, without regard to those collateral evidences by which its decisions may be modified and corrected." * . . . "Beyond question, every doubt which our reason may suggest in matters of religion is entitled to its due place in the examination of the evidences of religion; if we will treat it as a part only, and not the whole; if we will not insist on a positive solution of that which, it may be, is given us for another purpose than to be solved. It is reasonable to believe that, in matters of belief as well as of practice, God has not thought fit to annihilate the free will of man, but has permitted speculative difficulties to exist as the trial and the discipline of sharp and subtle intellects, as He has permitted moral temptations to form the trial and the discipline of strong and eager passions. . . . We do not

---

* *Bampton Lectures*, p. 157, Fourth Edition.

doubt that the conditions of our moral trial tend towards good, and not towards evil; that human nature, even in its fallen state, bears traces of the image of its Maker, and is fitted to be an instrument in His moral government. And we believe this, notwithstanding the existence of passions and appetites which, isolated and uncontrolled, appear to lead in an opposite direction. Is it then more reasonable to deny that a system of revealed religion, whose unquestionable tendency as a whole is to promote the glory of God and the welfare of mankind, can have proceeded from the same Author, merely because we may be unable to detect the same character in some of its minuter features, viewed apart from the system to which they belong?" *

Surely this is very different from denouncing all reasoning from human goodness to Divine as "illicit." To take a parallel case. The manufacture of gunpowder is a dangerous process, and, if carried on without due precautions, is very likely to lead to disastrous

* *Bampton Lectures*, p. 166, Fourth Edition.

consequences. Surely it is one thing to point out what precautions are necessary, and what evils are to be apprehended from the neglect of them, and another to forbid the manufacture altogether. Mr. Mill does not seem to see the difference.

We have now considered in detail all that part of Mr. Mill's book which is devoted to the examination of Sir W. Hamilton's chief and most characteristic doctrines — those which constitute the Philosophy of the Conditioned. The remainder of the work, which deals chiefly with subordinate questions of psychology and logic, contains much from which we widely dissent, but which we cannot at present submit to a special examination. Nor is it necessary, so far as Sir W. Hamilton's reputation is concerned, that we should do so. If the Philosophy of the Conditioned is really nothing better than the mass of crudities and blunders which Mr. Mill supposes it to be, the warmest admirers of Hamilton will do little in his behalf, even should they succeed in vindicating some of the minor details of his teaching. If, on the other hand, it can be shown, as we have attempted to show, that Mr. Mill is utterly incapable of dealing with Hamilton's philosophy in its higher branches, his readers may be left to judge for themselves whether he is implicitly to be trusted as regards the lower. In point of fact, they will do Mr. Mill no injustice, if they regard the above specimens as samples of his entire criticism. We gladly except, as of a far higher order, those chapters in which he is content with stating his own views; but in the perpetual baiting of Sir W. Hamilton, which occupies the greater part of the volume, we recognise, in general, the same captiousness and the same incompetence which we have so often had occasion to point out in the course of our previous remarks.

It is, we confess, an unpleasant and an invidious task, to pick to pieces, bit by bit, the work of an author of high reputation. But Mr. Mill has chosen to put the question on this issue, and he has left those who dissent from him no alternative but to follow his example. He has tasked all the resources of minute criticism to destroy piecemeal the reputation of one who has hitherto borne an honoured name in philosophy : he has no right to complain if the same measure is meted to himself :—

"Neque enim lex æquior ulla
Quam necis artifices arte perire sua."

But it is not so much the justice as the necessity of the case which we would plead as our excuse. Mr. Mill's method of criticism has reduced the question to a very narrow compass. Either Sir W. Hamilton, instead of being a great philosopher, is the veriest blunderer that ever put pen to paper, or the blunders are Mr. Mill's own. To those who accept the first of these alternatives it must always remain a marvel how Sir W. Hamilton could ever have acquired that reputation which compels even his critic to admit that "he alone, of our metaphysicians of this and the preceding generation, has acquired, merely as such, an European celebrity;" how he could have been designated by his illustrious opponent, Cousin, as the "greatest critic of our age," or described by the learned Brandis as "almost unparalleled in the profound knowledge of ancient and modern philosophy." The marvel may perhaps disappear, should it be the case, as we believe it to be, that the second alternative is the true one.

But even in this case, it should be borne in mind that the blow will by no means fall on Mr. Mill with the same weight with which he designed it to fall on the object of his criticism. Sir W. Hamilton had devoted his whole life to the study of metaphysics; he was probably more deeply read in that study than any of his contemporaries; and if all his reading could produce nothing better than the confusion and self-contradiction which Mr. Mill imputes to him, the result would be pitiable indeed. Mr. Mill, on the other hand, we strongly suspect, despises metaphysics too much to be at the pains of studying them at all, and seems to think that a critic is duly equipped for his task with that amount of knowledge which, like Dogberry's reading and writing, " comes by nature." His work has a superficial cleverness which, together with the author's previous reputation, will insure it a certain kind of popularity; but we venture to predict that its estimation by its readers will be in the inverse ratio to their knowledge of the subject. But Mr. Mill's general reputation rests on grounds quite distinct from his performances in metaphysics; and though we could hardly name one of his writings from whose main principles we do not dissent, there is hardly one which is not better fitted to sustain his character as a thinker than this last, in which the fatal charms of the goddess Necessity seem to have betrayed her champion into an unusual excess of polemical zeal, coupled, it must be added, with an unusual deficiency of philosophical knowledge.

POSTSCRIPT.

It was not till after the preceding pages had been sent to press that I became acquainted with a little work recently published under the title of *The Battle of the two Philosophies, by an Inquirer.* The author appears to have been a personal pupil of Sir W. Hamilton's, as well as a diligent student of his writings. At all events, he has "inquired" to some purpose, and obtained a far more intelligent knowledge of Hamilton's system than is exhibited by the majority of recent critics. It is gratifying to find many of my remarks confirmed by the concurrent testimony of so competent a witness. The following would have been noticed in their proper places had I been sooner acquainted with them.

Of the popular confusion between the *infinite* and the *indefinite*, noticed above, pp. 50, 112, "An Inquirer" observes:—

"If we could realise in thought infinite space, that conception would be a perfectly definite one; but the notion that is here offered us in its place, though it may be real, is certainly not definite; it is merely the conception of an indefinite extension. . . . . In truth, when we strive to think of infinite space, the nearest approach we can make to it is this notion of an indefinite space, which Mr. Mill has substituted for it. But these two conceptions are not only verbally, they are really wholly distinct. An indefinite space is a space of the extent of which we think vaguely, without knowing or without thinking where its boundaries are. Infinite space has certainly, and quite distinctly, no boundaries anywhere."—(Pp. 18–20.)

On Mr. Mill's strange distinction between the Divine Attributes, as some infinite and others absolute, the author's remarks are substantially in agreement with what has been said above on pp. 105-6.

"Mr. Mill argues that all the attributes of God cannot be infinite; but that some, as power, may be infinite; and some, as goodness and knowledge, must be absolute, because neither can knowledge be more than complete, nor goodness more than perfect. When we know all there is to be known, he says, knowledge has attained its utmost limit. But this is merely begging the whole question. If there be an Infinite Being, He cannot know all there is to be known unless He know Himself; and adequately to know what is infinite is to have infinite knowledge. The same thing would be true if there could be a Being whose power and duration only were infinite. 'The will,' he adds, 'is either entirely right, or wrong in different degrees: downwards there are as many gradations as we choose to distinguish; but upwards there is an ideal limit. Goodness can be imagined complete,— such that there can be no greater goodness beyond it.' . . . But a Being of infinite power and finite goodness would not be perfectly good, because His power would not be wholly, but only in part directed by His goodness. Nay, as that which is finite bears no proportion whatever to what is infinite: as, however great it be absolutely, it is still infinitely less than infinity, such a Being would be partly good and yet infinitely evil, which is absurd in reason and impossible in fact."—(Pp. 24, 25.)

The following estimate of Mr. Mill's merits as a metaphysician coincides with that which, contrary to my expectation, I found forced upon myself after a careful examination of his book.—(See above, Pp. 62, 182.)

"We cannot but think that Mr. Mill in this, his first work in pure metaphysics, has disappointed just expectation. In leaving the fields of practical philosophy, he seems to have left his genius behind him. Even the peculiar 'cunning of his right hand' —even his unexcelled logical power avails him little, so continually does he fail to see distinctly the conception with which he is fencing. . . . As long as he is applying given principles to the solution of practical questions; as long as he has to do with the process of an argument, he proves himself a most able instructor and guide. But when he has to grapple with a metaphysical problem, it almost invariably arrives that the central, the metaphysical difficulty, escapes him."—(Pp. 78-80.)

www.ingramcontent.com/pod-product-compliance
Lightning Source LLC
Chambersburg PA
CBHW030820190426
43197CB00036B/639